Dispensationalism

Rightly Dividing the People of God?

KEITH A. MATHISON

P U B L I S H I N G
P.O. BOX 817 • PHILLIPSBURG • NEW JERSEY 08865-0817

Scripture quotations are from the New American Standard Bible. Copyright by the Lockman Foundation 1960, 1962, 1963, 1968, 1971, 1973, 1975, 1977.

Printed in the United States of America

Library of Congress Cataloging-in-Publication Data

Mathison, Keith A., 1967-
    Dispensationalism : rightly dividing the people of God? / Keith A. Mathison.
        p.   cm.
    Includes bibliographical references and index.
    ISBN 0-87552-359-5
    1. Dispensationalism—Controversial literature. 2. Reformed Church—Doctrines. I. Title.
BT157.M38 1995
230'.046—dc20   95-11896

Dispensationalism

*Rightly Dividing the
People of God?*

To my wife, Tricia:
Every so often God creates someone
to remind us of the beauty of paradise
and to give us a foretaste of the beauty of heaven.

Contents

Preface

"I believe in the pretribulation rapture and in dispensationalism because all of the famous prophecy scholars teach it."

It was those words, which I heard on Christian radio one afternoon, that finally convinced me to write this book. The topic of the talk show was the rapture, which prompted dozens of phone calls from listeners. One caller, a middle-aged woman, was firmly convinced that pretribulationism and dispensationalism are true. When asked why she believed as she did, she responded with the words quoted above. Essentially she believed what her favorite authors taught. And I could not help wondering how many other people would have responded the same way.

The decision to write this book was not an easy one. Books like this inevitably offend some people. There is always the risk of misinterpreting others' beliefs, and there are temptations of pride, arrogance, and unkindness. So why would a Christian decide to write a book critical of a system of theology cherished by many godly men and women? There are two reasons.

First, as Christians our sole authority for doctrine is Scripture. We must not base our beliefs on fallible teachers, regardless of how popular they may be. The woman who called the radio station meant well, but there was a problem with her method of forming beliefs. Our method must be that of the Bereans spoken of in Acts 17:10–11. Although the apostle Paul himself was their teacher, the Bereans were praised for searching the Scriptures to see whether his teachings were true. If they searched the Scriptures to verify Paul's teaching, how much more should we search the Scriptures to verify the doctrines of our favorite teachers!

Second, I am writing this book because I am commanded to do unto others as I would have them do unto me. The dispensationalists I know desire to believe only what the Scriptures teach. That is also my desire. If dispensationalism is biblical, I want to know. And I trust that if it is unbiblical, most dispensationalists would want to know that too. All Christians are obliged to believe and teach what is biblical, and to reject what is not.

I would like to thank several individuals whose help with this project was invaluable. David Scott, Darren Edgington, Larry Lain, and Rick Bartley each read the manuscript in its entirety and offered many helpful suggestions. Without their constructive criticism, this book would never have been completed. Of course whatever defects and shortcomings remain are entirely my responsibility.

This book is addressed to any and all honest believers in our Lord Jesus Christ, who desire to love the Lord with all of their heart and soul and mind; to believe and teach only the truth regardless of the cost; and to search the Scriptures diligently to discover that truth. To these men and women this book is humbly offered in the hope that it will be of some small service to the body of Christ.

PART 1

Introduction

Defining Dispensationalism

Much of the confusion and ignorance surrounding the subject of dispensationalism is due to misconceptions and inaccurate definitions. As we shall see, much time is wasted in discussions of irrelevant issues simply because important terms have not been well defined. The purpose of this chapter, therefore, is to define clearly what dispensationalism is and what it is not.

Dispensationalism is too often defined in terms of its lowest common denominator and thus is not adequately distinguished from other systems of theology. For example, Stanley Toussaint defines dispensationalism as the theological system that "recognizes various administrations or economies in [the] outworking of God's plan in history."[1] This definition omits anything that is unique to dispensationalism. Virtually every system of Christian theology recognizes various administrations or economies within God's plan, yet it would be inaccurate to claim that all of these systems are dispensational. Dispensationalism must be defined in terms of its unique essence, namely that which distinguishes it from other systems of theology.

Some examples may prove helpful. Would it suffice to define covenant theology as the system of doctrine that recognizes various covenants within God's plan? No. Dispensationalists and others also recognize the biblical covenants, but they cannot be regarded as covenant theologians. Would it be enough to define Baptist theology as that which believes in the importance of baptism? Of course not. Other systems of theology also recognize the importance of baptism. Could charismatic theology be adequately defined as the system of theology that believes in the work of the Holy Spirit? Again the answer is no. Every system of Christian theology recognizes the work of the Holy Spirit.

A system of theology cannot be amply defined in terms of doctrines it shares with virtually every other system of theology. Thus it is not enough to say that dispensationalism is the system of theology that recognizes different dispensations. Charles Ryrie, an eminent dispensationalist, agrees that "a man can believe in dispensations, and even see them in relation to progressive revelation without being a dispensationalist."[2]

Some have argued that the essence of dispensationalism is premillennialism. That would make it at least part of the definition of dispensationalism. But Ryrie disagrees, noting that "being a premillennialist does not necessarily make one a dispensationalist."[3] Indeed, premillennialism has existed in one form or another since the first century, but dispensationalism dates from only about 1830. Moreover, premillennialism is the belief that Christ will return *before* the millennium. Dispensationalism is a system of theology that encompasses much more than a particular view of the millennium. Premillennialism, therefore, cannot be equated with dispensationalism.

If dispensationalism is not simply the recognition of various dispensations, and if it is not premillennialism, then what is it? What distinguishes dispensationalism from other systems of theology? Charles Ryrie offers this answer:

The essence of dispensationalism, then, is the distinction between Israel and the Church. This grows out of the dispensationalists' consistent employment of normal or plain interpretation, and it reflects an understanding of the basic purpose of God in all His dealings with mankind as that of glorifying Himself through salvation and other purposes as well.[4]

In this definition of dispensationalism, Ryrie makes three assertions:

1. First and most importantly, the essence of dispensationalism is the distinction between Israel and the church.
2. This distinction is the result of consistently literal interpretation.
3. This distinction reflects the understanding that God's primary purpose is to glorify Himself.

Let us examine these claims in reverse order.

God's Primary Purpose, to Glorify Himself. Until very recently, dispensationalists maintained that they alone understood God's ultimate purpose to be His own glory. Other theological systems, especially Reformed theology, were accused of teaching that God's ultimate purpose is the redemption of man. Dispensationalism was therefore said to be God-centered, while Reformed theology was allegedly man-centered.[5]

This characterization of Reformed theology cannot stand up to the facts. The second chapter of the Westminster Confession of Faith, which was completed in 1646, and which was the last classic Reformed confession, declares that God is working *all* things for His own glory. Chapter 3 declares that predestination is for the manifestation of God's glory. And in chapter 4, creation is said to be for the manifestation of God's glory. The glory of God is a dominant theme throughout the entire confession. It is also the dominant theme of the Westminster Catechisms. In fact, the answer to the first question of the Shorter Catechism states that the chief end of man is "to glorify God, and to enjoy him for ever."

In addition, numerous Reformed theologians have expressly affirmed that very point. Charles Hodge wrote in his *Systematic Theology* that the glory of God is the purpose "of the universe as a whole; of the external world or works of nature; [and] of the plan of redemption."[6] A. A. Hodge agrees that the glory of God is "the chief end of God in all his purposes and works of Providence and Redemption."[7] Louis Berkhof concurred: "The final aim is the glory of God. Even the salvation of men is subordinate to this. That the glory of God is the highest purpose of the electing grace is made very emphatic in Eph. 1:6, 12, 14."[8]

Reformed theology clearly recognizes that God's ultimate purpose is His own glory. It also recognizes that God has many subordinate purposes, one of which is the redemption of man. There is obviously no basis for the claim that dispensationalism alone sees God's own glory as the ultimate purpose of all things. Reformed theologians and Reformed confessions declared that truth hundreds of years before dispensationalism existed.[9] Both dispensationalism and Reformed theology understand that God's ultimate and primary purpose is His own glory, out of which flow many subordinate purposes.

Consistently Literal Interpretation. Ryrie's second assertion is that dispensationalism employs consistently literal biblical interpretation. Two main points in connection with this claim deserve mention. First, despite their efforts, dispensationalists have never been entirely consistent in interpretating the Bible literally. For example, C. I. Scofield wrote, "It is then permitted—while holding firmly the historical verity—reverently to spiritualize the historical Scriptures."[10] John Walvoord, another prominent dispensationalist, insists that when an Old Testament prophecy refers to Israel, it must mean the literal nation of Israel; but when the same Old Testament prophecy speaks of other nations, such as Assyria or Philistia, it only refers to the land once inhabited by these nations. Whoever may be inhabiting these lands may fulfill these prophecies.[11] This is not consistent literalism.

The fact is that nobody can be absolutely literal in his interpretation of Scripture. The Bible itself will not allow it. There are some insurmountable scriptural problems that occur if one attempts to be consistently literal in his approach to interpretation.

Consider one example. Dispensationalists understand Ezekiel 40–48 to be a prophecy of the future millennial temple and the worship that will occur there. The problem is that there are numerous passages in these chapters that depict the practice of animal sacrifices (40:38–43; 42:13; 43:18–27; 44:11, 27, 29; 45:13–25; 46:2–7, 11–15, 20). These verses should not be interpreted literally and placed in a future millennium. Hebrews 10:10–18 forbids it: "Now where there is forgiveness of these things, there is no longer any offering for sin" (v. 18). According to Hebrews the purpose of the sacrificial system has been fulfilled. The once-for-all sacrificial death of Christ has *forever* ended the offering of animal sacrifices.

Some dispensationalists answer that these animal sacrifices will merely be memorials offered in remembrance of Christ's death. But that is not what Ezekiel *literally* says. Ezekiel calls these offerings "sin offerings" (40:39; 43:19, 21, 22, 25; 44:27, 29; 45:17, 22, 23, 25; 46:20). And Hebrews 10:18 says that after Christ's death there is no more offering for sin. Moreover, the offerings in Ezekiel 45:15, 17 are *literally* said to make atonement:

> ". . . and one sheep from each flock of two hundred from the watering places of Israel—for a grain offering, for a burnt offering, and for peace offerings, *to make atonement* for them," declares the Lord GOD. . . .
> "And it shall be the prince's part to provide the burnt offerings, the grain offerings, and the libations, at the feasts, on the new moons, and on the sabbaths, at all the appointed feasts of the house of Israel; he shall provide the sin offering, the grain offering, the burnt

offering, and the peace offerings, *to make atonement* for the house of Israel."

It is impossible to interpret Ezekiel 40–48 in a strictly literal manner in reference to a future millennium without denying the clear teaching of Hebrews on the final sacrifice of Christ. To do so introduces a contradiction into Scripture that is easily avoided by seeing Ezekiel's descriptions as figurative. If the Old Testament prophets could prophesy about Christ figuratively in terms of the Levitical sacrifices, why could Ezekiel not have "prophesied the church age [figuratively] in terms of the Old Testament religious system with which ancient Israel was familiar?"[12] Jesus did not come as a literal lamb with four legs and wool, and neither will a future millennium come with literal bloody sacrifices. Dispensationalists cannot be consistently literal in their interpretation of this passage. That would demand the restoration of bloody, atoning (not memorial) animal sacrifices, which is impossible now that Christ has offered Himself as the final sacrifice. Dispensationalists must realize that context determines whether a given passage of Scripture is literal or figurative.

The Distinction Between Israel and the Church. The only one of Ryrie's three distinctives of dispensationalism that has always been acknowledged as true is the distinction between Israel and the church. The particular dispensationalist understanding of this distinction is the heart of that system of theology. Dispensationalism may, therefore, be defined as that system of theology which sees a fundamental distinction between Israel and the church. This distinction is the cornerstone of dispensational theology. Other doctrines, which are often considered to be distinctively dispensational, rest upon this doctrine of the church. With this definition clearly in mind, much of the confusion that often surrounds this topic may be avoided.

NOTES

1. Stanley Toussaint, "A Biblical Defense of Dispensationalism," *Walvoord: A Tribute*, ed. Donald K. Campbell (Chicago: Moody Press, 1982), 82–83.

2. Charles Ryrie, *Dispensationalism Today* (Chicago: Moody Press, 1965), 44. A revised and expanded edition of *Dispensationalism Today* (Chicago: Moody Press, 1995) has just been released as this book undergoes preparation for press. Ryrie has updated his treatment to include discussions of progressive dispensationalism and of recent criticisms of dispensationalism. His essential views remain unchanged.

3. Ibid.

4. Ibid., 47.

5. Ibid., 98–105.

6. Charles Hodge, *Systematic Theology*, 3 vols. (Grand Rapids: Eerdmans, 1989 [1872]), 1:567.

7. A. A. Hodge, *Outlines of Theology* (Carlisle, Pa.: Banner of Truth, 1972 [1860]), 244.

8. Louis Berkhof, *Systematic Theology* (Grand Rapids: Eerdmans, 1939), 115.

9. It must also be noted that dispensationalists have made statements that seem to contradict their own claim. For example, Lewis Sperry Chafer declared that the church "is the supreme purpose of God in the universe" (*Systematic Theology*, 8 vols. [Dallas: Dallas Seminary Press, 1947], 4:54).

10. C. I. Scofield, *Scofield Bible Correspondence Course* (Chicago: Moody Bible Institute, 1907), 45–46.

11. John F. Walvoord, *The Nations in Prophecy* (Grand Rapids: Zondervan, 1967), 163.

12. Curtis I. Crenshaw and Grover E. Gunn III, *Dispensationalism Today, Yesterday, and Tomorrow*, rev. ed. (Memphis: Footstool Publications, 1989), 222.

Dispensationalism and History

The History of Dispensationalism

In order to understand the place of dispensationalism in Christian theology we must briefly examine its history.[1] Dispensationalism arose in the early nineteenth century in Great Britain within the Brethren movement, which was led by men such as John Nelson Darby, Samuel P. Tregelles, and Charles Henry Mackintosh. They and other Brethren leaders produced volumes of expositional works, which influenced many prominent Christians in the United States, including D. L. Moody, James H. Brookes, and C. I. Scofield.

The Brethren influence in the United States produced the Bible Conference Movement, starting with the Niagara Bible Conferences in the 1870s. The movement soon spread to other parts of the country. In 1909 C. I. Scofield published his now famous *Scofield Reference Bible,* which placed the teachings of the conferences and the Brethren into the hands of the general public. The system of theology outlined in the notes of his study Bible soon became known as "dispensationalism."

Among those influenced by Scofield was an evangelist named Lewis Sperry Chafer. Eventually Chafer would establish the Evangelical Theological College, which later changed its name to Dallas Theological Seminary. The role of Dallas Seminary in the growth of dispensationalism can hardly be overstated. The seminary has produced several giants within the dispensational tradition: John F. Walvoord, Charles C. Ryrie, and J. Dwight Pentecost, to name a few. Following the tradition of their Brethren predecessors, these men have churned out volumes of literature and influenced countless thousands of Christians. In the process they have spread dispensationalism around the globe.

Is Dispensationalism Well Rooted in History?

Dispensationalism is a fairly new development in theology. But how important is the relative newness of this doctrine? After all, we know that the Bible alone is our authority in judging truth from error. Does it matter that dispensationalism is a recent doctrinal development?

Among dispensationalists we find conflicting answers to that question. Sometimes conflicting opinions appear in the writings of a single author.

In his book *The Basis of the Premillennial Faith,* Charles Ryrie says that the historical argument is of the "utmost importance."[2] However, in *Dispensationalism Today,* he vehemently criticizes those who use the historical argument as if it were "partly valid."[3] Which is it? Is the historical argument of the utmost importance or is it not even partly valid? It certainly cannot be both.

The importance of the historical argument seems often to depend on the particular doctrine under consideration. Dispensationalists enjoy pointing out the historical antiquity of premillennialism. But when it comes to other doctrines, those which first appeared around 1830, dispensationalists downplay the significance of the historical question. Historical arguments are not the final test for the truthfulness of any doctrine. Scripture is our sole authority for both doctrine and practice. Yet the history of a doctrine can be highly relevant. We have much more reason to be confident of a doctrine such as the Trinity, which has been taught since the first centuries of the church age, than of a doctrine first taught 150 years ago. As a rule, Christians should be cautious about accepting any doctrine that has never been taught in the history of the church.

One problem with tracing the antiquity of dispensationalism is that dispensationalism is often poorly defined, as we saw earlier. If it is defined as a system that recognizes different dispensations, then it can be found anywhere in church history, even in the church fathers. But, again, this definition of dispensationalism is inadequate.

Ryrie's use of the historical argument will illustrate the problem. After stating that the recognition of different dispensations is *neither* the essence of dispensationalism *nor* even a major part of it, Ryrie seeks to prove that the early church fathers held to an undeveloped form of dispensationalism because they recognized different dispensations.[4] In other words, he argues that believing "A" does not make one a dispensationalist, then argues that the church fathers were basically dispensationalists because they believed in "A." It is as if Ryrie is saying that being yellow does not make something a banana, but because these lemons are yellow, they must therefore be bananas. This kind of argument renders almost all of chapter 4 of his book *Dispensationalism Today* irrelevant. It also renders irrelevant any work that attempts to find dispensationalism in the early church by citing church fathers who believed in different dispensations.

Ryrie himself correctly identified the essence of dispensationalism as the distinction between Israel and the church: church-age saints form one body and all other saints form another. If someone wants to demonstrate that the early church held to an undeveloped form of dispensationalism, he must find in the church fathers this doctrine of two bodies of saints. The main reason that no such attempt is made to find the essence of dispensationalism in the early church is that it simply is not there. The *essential* doctrine of dispensationalism cannot be found prior to the nineteenth century.

The early church fathers are almost unanimous in their identification of the church and Israel.[5] One example will suffice. Justin Martyr (A.D. 110–165) is often quoted by dispensationalists attempting to prove the early history of premillennialism. He was a premillennialist, but he was certainly not a dispensationalist. In chapter 135 of his *Dialogue with Trypho,* Justin writes, "As, therefore, Christ is the Israel and the Jacob, even so we, who have been quarried out from the bowels of Christ, are the true Israelitic race." Here is Justin, a gentile church leader, speaking to Trypho, a Jew, and claiming that the church is the true Israel.

Neither Justin nor any of the other church fathers were dispensationalists. They did not even hold to an "undeveloped" form of dispensationalism. The Fathers taught that the true church is the true Israel.

Even so, we must not base our doctrine upon the church fathers. We must build our understanding upon the teaching of the inerrant Word of God.

NOTES

1. For a more thorough examination of the history of dispensationalism, see Clarence Bass, *Backgrounds to Dispensationalism* (Grand Rapids: Eerdmans, 1960).
2. Charles C. Ryrie, *The Basis of the Premillennial Faith* (Neptune, N.J.: Loizeaux Brothers, 1953), 33.
3. Charles C. Ryrie, *Dispensationalism Today* (Chicago: Moody Press, 1965), 13.
4. Ibid., 67–70.
5. See for example: Papias, *Fragment* 6; *I Clement* 3:1; 29:1–30:1; *II Clement* 2:1–3; 3:5; *Barnabas* 2:4–6, 9; 3:6; 4:6–7; 5:2, 7; Hermas, *Similitudes* 9.16.7; 9.15.4; 9.12.1–13.2; *The Didache* 14:2, 3; Justin Martyr, *Dialogue with Trypho* 119–20, 123, 125.

PART 2

The Dispensational Doctrine of the Church

The Doctrine of the Church

The dispensational doctrine of the church distinguishes that system of theology from all others. As we have seen, it is the essential doctrine of dispensationalism. Ryrie himself makes this point: "Ecclesiology, or the doctrine of the Church, is the touchstone of dispensationalism."[1]

Though the dispensational doctrine of the church is complex, its essential features can be summarized under seven propositions.

1. God has two distinct programs in history, one for Israel and one for the church.
2. The church does not fulfill or take over any of Israel's promises or purposes.
3. The church age is a "mystery," and thus no Old Testament prophecies foresaw it.

4. The present church age is a "parenthesis" or "intercalation" during which God has temporarily suspended His primary purpose with Israel.
5. The church age began at Pentecost and will end at the pretribulation rapture of the church before Christ's second coming.
6. The church, or body of Christ, consists only of those believers saved between Pentecost and the rapture.
7. The church as the body of Christ, therefore, does not include Old Testament believers.

These doctrines can be found consistently throughout the writings of the most prominent dispensationalist scholars, as we are about to see. In order to demonstrate that these are not the teachings of a few obscure dispensationalists, this chapter will allow the leading dispensationalists of the twentieth century to express their views in their own words on each of the seven propositions.

1. God has two distinct programs in history, one for Israel and one for the church.

Lewis Sperry Chafer. "The distinction between the purpose for Israel and the purpose for the Church is about as important as that which exists between the two testaments."[2]
John F. Walvoord. "Dispensational ecclesiology defines the church as a distinct body of saints in the present age having its own divine purpose and destiny and differing from the saints of the past or future ages."[3]
J. Dwight Pentecost. "THE DIVINE PURPOSE: Israel—the earthly promises in the covenants; Church—the heavenly promises in the gospel."[4]
Charles C. Ryrie. "This is why the dispensationalist recognizes two purposes of God and insists in maintaining the distinction between Israel and the church."[5]

2. The church does not fulfill or take over any of Israel's promises or purposes.

Lewis Sperry Chafer. "That the Christian now inherits the distinctive Jewish promises is not taught in Scripture."[6]

John F. Walvoord. "The whole tenor of the chapter [Romans 11] is against either the idea that Israel has lost all future hope of fulfillment of their promises through cancellation or that the church has received these promises and Israel is disinherited."[7]

J. Dwight Pentecost. "Since the church today is composed of both Jews and Gentiles without national distinction it would be impossible for the church to fulfill God's promises made exclusively to the nation of Israel."[8]

Charles C. Ryrie. "The church is not fulfilling in any sense the promises to Israel."[9]

3. The church age is a "mystery," and thus no Old Testament prophecies foresaw it.

Lewis Sperry Chafer. "The first prediction relative to the true Church was uttered by Christ, being recorded in Matthew 16:18."[10]

John F. Walvoord. ". . . dispensationalists have regarded the present age as a parenthesis unexpected and without specific prediction in the Old Testament."[11]

J. Dwight Pentecost. "It has been illustrated how this whole age existed in the mind of God without having been revealed in the Old Testament."[12] "The church is a mystery, unrevealed in the Old Testament."[13]

Charles C. Ryrie. "The Church is a mystery in the sense that it was completely unrevealed in the Old Testament and now revealed in the New Testament."[14]

4. The present church age is a parenthesis or intercalation during which God has temporarily suspended His primary purpose with Israel.

Lewis Sperry Chafer.

In fact, the new, hitherto unrevealed purpose of God in the outcalling of a heavenly people from Jews and

Gentiles is so divergent with respect to the divine purpose toward Israel, which purpose preceded it and
will yet follow it, that the term *parenthetical*, commonly
employed to describe the new age-purpose, is inaccurate. A parenthetical portion sustains some direct or
indirect relation to that which goes before or that which
follows; but the present age-purpose is not thus related
and therefore is more properly termed an *intercalation*.[15]

John F. Walvoord. "The evidence if interpreted literally
leads inevitably to the parenthesis doctrine."[16]
J. Dwight Pentecost. "The church is manifestly an inter-
ruption of God's program for Israel."[17]
Charles C. Ryrie. "The Church age is not seen in God's
program for Israel. It is an intercalation."[18]

5. *The church age began at Pentecost and will end at the pretribulation
rapture.*

Lewis Sperry Chafer.

The principle emphasis in the New Testament is on the
church as an organism, a living union of all true believers in Christ. This is the distinctive truth that is pre-
sented beginning with the day of Pentecost, with the
advent of the Spirit, and concluding with the coming
of Christ for His church, in which the church will be
caught up out of the world and taken to heaven.[19]

John F. Walvoord. ". . . the body of Christ which properly
began on the Day of Pentecost and culminates in the translation
of the true church."[20]
J. Dwight Pentecost. "It is after the rejection of the Cross
that the church had its inception in Acts 2."[21] "The present age,
in respect to the true church, terminates with the translation of
the church into the Lord's presence."[22]

Charles C. Ryrie. "The Church did not begin until the day of Pentecost and will be removed from this world at the rapture which precedes the Second Coming of Christ."[23]

6. *The church, or body of Christ, consists only of those believers saved between Pentecost and the rapture.*

Lewis Sperry Chafer. "The body of Christ contrasts sharply with the relationship of God to Israel and Gentiles in the Old Testament and is a unique situation limited to the present age."[24]

John F. Walvoord. "The church as the body of Christ is therefore a new entity, and the term *ecclesia* when used in this sense is used only of saints of the present dispensation."[25]

J. Dwight Pentecost. "The true church is composed of all those in this age who have received Christ as Savior."[26]

Charles C. Ryrie. ". . . the Church is a distinct body of saints in this age."[27]

7. *The church, or body of Christ, therefore does not include Old Testament believers.*

Lewis Sperry Chafer. "By Spirit baptism the believer is placed into the body of Christ in the living union of all true believers in the present age."[28]

John F. Walvoord. "The expression 'in Christ' is uniformly used in the New Testament, wherever it has theological meaning, as a reference to those who have been baptized by the Spirit into the body of Christ, and is never used in reference to saints before the Day of Pentecost."[29]

J. Dwight Pentecost. "There is a distinction between the true church and true or spiritual Israel. Prior to Pentecost there were saved individuals, but there was no church, and they were a part of spiritual Israel, not the church."[30]

Charles C. Ryrie. "Nevertheless, dispensationalism insists that the people of God who have been baptized into the Body of Christ and who thus form the Church are distinct from saints of other days or even of a future time."[31]

These leading spokesmen confirm that the dispensational doctrine of the church consists of these seven propositions. That doctrine is *the* distinguishing teaching of dispensationalism, and this system of theology stands or falls with it.

Unfortunately that doctrine is often stated in confusing terms. One source of confusion is the ambiguous use of the terms "Israel" and "church." If "Israel" is used in three different ways within one paragraph, that is bound to cause confusion, as can be seen in Ryrie's attempt to prove a distinction between Israel and the church.

> The church stands distinct from Israel and did not begin until the Day of Pentecost, and thus did not exist in the Old Testament period. . . . The distinction between Israel and the church is verified by several facts. (1) In the New Testament natural Israel and Gentiles are contrasted *after* the church was clearly established (Acts 3:12; 4:8, 10; 5:21, 31, 35; 21:19). (2) Natural Israel and the church are clearly distinguished, showing that the church is not Israel (I Cor. 10:32). The apostles' distinction would be meaningless if Israel were the same as the church. (3) Galatians 6:16 provides no clear proof that the church is equated with Israel.[32]

Has Ryrie proved something distinctively dispensational? He claims to verify the distinction between Israel (undefined) and the church. But in point 1 Ryrie changes the subject by inserting the word "natural" in reference to Israel, which refers to the nation of unbelieving, physical Jews.

What relevance is there in saying that "natural" Israel is distinct from Gentiles either before or after Pentecost? Nobody, dispensational or otherwise, disputes that. Obviously the nation of Israel is distinct from the gentile nations. Israel is not equivalent to the United States for example, nor is it equivalent to any other gentile nation. No Reformed non-dispensationalist ever asserted such a thing. The obvious distinction between the nation of Israel and gentile nations does not in any way prove Ryrie's point.

Ryrie's addition of the word "natural" in point 2 renders that argument irrelevant as well. Again, nobody is arguing that the church is equivalent to "natural" unbelieving Israel. *Natural* Israel is a nation of physical Jews who live in the land of Palestine. The obvious fact that the nation of Israel is distinct from the church proves nothing. *All* nations, including Israel, are distinct from the church.

It is difficult to understand why Ryrie included point 3 in his proof. In context, what he says is this: "The distinction between Israel and the church is verified" because "Galatians 6:16 provides no clear proof that the church is equated with Israel." But how can the fact that Galatians 6:16 proves nothing "verify" the distinction between Israel and the church? If I were to argue that either amillennialism or postmillennialism is *verified* by the fact that Revelation 20 does not *clearly* teach premillennialism, I would be arguing from silence. Likewise, if Galatians 6:16 is unclear, then it doesn't *prove* either position to be true. We must look elsewhere for proof.

Not one of Ryrie's three proofs actually make his point. He needs to demonstrate the distinction between Israel and the church *in the sense that dispensationalism understands those terms.* It does no good to prove a distinction that is generally accepted but irrelevant to the question at hand.

The real point of disagreement centers on the relationship between believers in the church age and believers in other ages. Dispensationalism teaches that they are two distinct bodies. According to dispensationalism, believers who died prior to Pentecost are not part of the body of Christ, the church. Reformed theology teaches that the believers of all ages are part of the one body of Christ. This is the heart of the debate between dispensationalists and nondispensationalists. Is there one body of believers or are there two?

NOTES

1. Charles C. Ryrie, *Dispensationalism Today* (Chicago: Moody Press, 1965), 132.
2. Lewis Sperry Chafer, *Systematic Theology,* 8 vols. (Dallas: Dallas

Seminary Press, 1947), 4:47.
3. John F. Walvoord, *The Millennial Kingdom* (Grand Rapids: Zondervan, 1959), 224.
4. J. Dwight Pentecost, *Things to Come* (Grand Rapids: Zondervan, 1958), 201.
5. Ryrie, *Dispensationalism Today*, 96.
6. Chafer, *Systematic Theology*, 4:316.
7. Walvoord, *Millennial Kingdom*, 172.
8. J. Dwight Pentecost, *Thy Kingdom Come* (Wheaton: Victor Books, 1990), 173.
9. Charles C. Ryrie, *The Basis of the Premillennial Faith* (Neptune, N.J.: Loizeaux Brothers, 1953), 136.
10. Chafer, *Systematic Theology*, 4:374.
11. Walvoord, *Millennial Kingdom*, 227.
12. Pentecost, *Things to Come*, 137.
13. Ibid., 193.
14. Ryrie, *Basis of the Premillennial Faith*, 136.
15. Chafer, *Systematic Theology*, 4:41.
16. Walvoord, *Millennial Kingdom*, 230.
17. Pentecost, *Things to Come*, 201.
18. Ryrie, *Basis of the Premillennial Faith*, 136.
19. Lewis Sperry Chafer and John F. Walvoord, *Major Bible Themes*, rev. ed. (Grand Rapids: Zondervan, 1974), 236.
20. John F. Walvoord, *The Church in Prophecy* (Grand Rapids: Zondervan, 1964), 24.
21. Pentecost, *Things to Come*, 201.
22. Ibid., 156.
23. Ryrie, *Basis of the Premillennial Faith*, 136.
24. Chafer and Walvoord, *Major Bible Themes*, 278.
25. Walvoord, *Millennial Kingdom*, 226.
26. Pentecost, *Things to Come*, 199.
27. Ryrie, *Basis of the Premillennial Faith*, 136.
28. Chafer and Walvoord, *Major Bible Themes*, 110.
29. Walvoord, *Millennial Kingdom*, 280.
30. Pentecost, *Things to Come*, 199.
31. Ryrie, *Dispensationalism Today*, 137.
32. Charles C. Ryrie, *Basic Theology* (Wheaton: Victor, 1982), 399.

CHAPTER 4

The Doctrine of the Church Examined

In the previous chapter we explained the dispensational doctrine of the church in terms of seven propositions. The purpose of this chapter is to examine the first five of those propositions in light of Scripture. Because of the significance of the last two propositions, they will be treated in greater detail in chapter 5.

1. God has two distinct programs in history, one for Israel and one for the church.

Whether this proposition is true depends on how "Israel" and "church" are defined. If "Israel" means national, unbelieving, political Israel, and the "church" means believers, then obviously there are different purposes for the two. If however "Israel" refers to true Israel and "church" refers to believers of this age or of all ages, then they cannot have two different programs.

Scripture teaches that all believers of all ages have one God (Deut. 4: 35, 39; 6:4; Eph. 4:6), one Savior and Lord Jesus Christ (Eph. 4:5; 1 Cor. 8:6; 1 Tim. 2:5), one way of salvation (John 14:6; Acts 4:12), and one eternal destiny (1 Thess. 4:17; Rev. 20:12). The believers of all ages are one body (Eph. 4:4), one bride (Rev. 21:9–14), one household (Eph. 2:19), and one flock (John 10:16). There is one purpose for all believers, and that is to glorify God (1 Cor. 10:31; Rom. 11:36).

2. The church does not fulfill or take over any of Israel's promises or purposes.

The second proposition follows logically from the first. If we were to understand Israel as simply the unbelieving nation and the church as believers, or if we were to regard them as two completely separate bodies of believers, then we could assume this second proposition to be true. If, however, the believers in Old Testament Israel and in the New Testament are one body, then it would make sense that the promises to the one might be fulfilled in the other. When we turn to the Scriptures, we see that promises originally made to the literal nation of Israel are in fact being fulfilled today in the church.

The Abrahamic Covenant

The Abrahamic covenant was initially fulfilled by the physical descendants of Abraham, but it has its true and complete fulfillment in Jesus Christ and His church. It will have its ultimate eternal fulfillment in the new heavens and new earth.

Dispensationalists argue that the Abrahamic covenant has never been fulfilled completely by the physical descendants of Abraham. But is that true?

Scripture teaches us several things about the fulfillment of the Abrahamic covenant. God has already fulfilled the promises He made specifically to Abraham, that He would make Abraham a great nation (Gen. 12:2). Did God not fulfill

this promise? Was not Israel a great nation in history, especially under David and Solomon? God promised Abraham that
his descendants would be as "the dust of the earth" (Gen.
13:16). In 2 Chronicles 1:9 Solomon prays, "Now, O LORD God,
Thy promise to my father David is fulfilled; for Thou hast
made me king over a people as numerous as the dust of the
earth." Abraham was promised that his descendants would
be as numerous as the stars of the heavens (Gen. 15:5). This
promise was also fulfilled (1 Chron. 27:23).[1]

God also promised Abraham that his seed would possess the land of Palestine and more (Gen. 12:7; 13:15; etc.). In
Genesis 15:18 we read, "On that day the LORD made a covenant with Abram, saying, 'To your descendants I have given
this land, From the river of Egypt as far as the great river, the
river Euphrates.'" If we compare this promise to 1 Kings 4:20–
21, we notice some striking parallels. First Kings 4:20 reminds
readers of the promise recorded in Genesis 22:17. Then verse
21 says, "Now Solomon ruled over all the kingdoms from the
River to the land of the Philistines and to the border of Egypt."
The author of 1 Kings is obviously referring back to the promise in Genesis, which his readers and hearers would know by
heart.

There are numerous other passages in the Old Testament
that tell us God has already fulfilled the land promises given to
Israel (Josh. 11:23; 21:41–45; Neh. 9:21–25). Joshua 21:43–45 explicitly declares that *all* the land that God promised Israel was
given to them: "So the LORD gave Israel all the land which He
had sworn to give to their fathers, and they possessed it and
lived in it. . . . Not one of the good promises which the LORD had
made to the house of Israel failed; all came to pass." God fulfilled the promises that He made to Abraham.

In the New Testament we discover something more. We
learn that in the ultimate sense Jesus Christ is *the* Seed of Abraham
(Gal. 3:16). We also learn that *all* who are in Christ are also
Abraham's seed and coheirs of the promises made to Abraham
(v. 29). We learn that the land promise has been expanded. It no
longer includes only the terrain from the Euphrates to Egypt. It

now includes the entire world (Rom. 4:13). We will not only inherit Palestine as coheirs with Christ; we will inherit the earth (Matt. 5:5).

The New Covenant

The new covenant is perhaps the clearest example of a promise made to national Israel that is now being fulfilled in and by the church. Dispensationalists have consistently taught that the church cannot fulfill the new covenant of Jeremiah 31.[2] For example J. Dwight Pentecost argues, "It should be clear from a survey of the passages already cited that this covenant [the new covenant] was made with Israel, the physical seed of Abraham according to the flesh, and with them alone."[3] More recently Pentecost has written that "the Church cannot be presently fulfilling the New Covenant."[4] John Walvoord agrees, saying that "the New Covenant is with Israel and awaits the second coming of Christ for its fulfillment."[5]

Dispensationalists insist that the church cannot fulfill the new covenant because such fulfillment would undermine the doctrine of premillennialism. "If the church fulfills this [new] Covenant, she may also fulfill the other covenants made with Israel and there is no need for an earthly millennium."[6]

But the church *is* fulfilling the Abrahamic covenant (Gal. 3:16, 29), and there is abundant scriptural evidence to demonstrate that the church is also fulfilling the new covenant.

During the Last Supper with His disciples, Jesus links the institution of the new covenant to His coming death on the cross (Luke 22:20). Paul the apostle declares that he himself is a servant of the new covenant in 2 Corinthians 3:4–6. In the book of Hebrews we find undeniable proof that the new covenant is being fulfilled by the church in this age (Heb. 7:22; 8:6–13; 9:15; 10:14–18, 29; 12:22–24). Hebrews 8:6–13 tells us that Jesus is the Mediator of the new covenant now. Verses 8–12 quote the prophecy of Jeremiah 31, demonstrating that both passages speak of one and the same new covenant. Hebrews teaches repeatedly that the old covenant has been abolished and that the new covenant has been inaugurated by Jesus Christ through the shedding of His blood.

The promises made to literal, physical Israelites were fulfilled by a literal, physical Israelite, Jesus the Messiah. He is *the* Seed of Abraham. What dispensationalism fails to grasp is that through union with Christ, *all* who are His by faith have become members of His body. Therefore, *all* who are in Him by faith, whether Old Testament believers or New Testament believers, are coheirs of the promises and the covenants. The covenantal promises do not require a future fulfillment by national Israel in order for God's Word to be true. The promises were typologically fulfilled by national Israel in the Old Testament (Josh. 21:43–45). They are now being fulfilled by the true Seed of Abraham, Jesus Christ (Gal. 3:16). And they are also being fulfilled in and by all who are united to Christ by faith (v. 29).

Though dispensationalists deny that the church can fulfill or is fulfilling promises made to the nation of Israel, Scripture teaches that Christians are coheirs of the promises made to Abraham and partakers of the new covenant. How is this possible? The answer is Jesus Christ. In Him all of God's promises find their true fulfillment (2 Cor. 1:20). And the church, through union with Him, shares in these promises.

3. The church age is a mystery, and thus no Old Testament prophecies foresaw it.

Dispensationalism teaches that the church age was completely unforeseen in the Old Testament and that it was not revealed until Jesus came. Though this is the unanimous verdict of traditional dispensationalism, it is contradicted by Scripture.

In Acts 3:24, the apostle Peter declares, "And likewise, all the prophets who have spoken, from Samuel and his successors onward, also announced these days." Peter spoke these words *after* Pentecost. Notice that he did not only say that this age was foreseen, but that it was announced by *all* the prophets. The Day of Pentecost, the very day dispensationalists mark as the beginning of the church age, was predicted in the prophecies of the Old Testament (Acts 2:16–17; cf. Joel 2:28). The Old Testament also predicts God's work of taking from among the Gentiles a people for Himself (Acts 15:13–17; cf. Amos 9:11–12).The dispensationalist claim that the church age was not seen in the prophecies of the Old Testament cannot be maintained. Scripture clearly tells us that *all* the prophets announced these days.

4. The present church age is a parenthesis or intercalation during which God has temporarily suspended His primary purpose with Israel.

If there were Old Testament prophecies of the church age as Acts 3:24 clearly demonstrates, then it cannot legitimately be argued that this age is a "parenthesis." God has not "suspended" His purpose for national Israel. He has fulfilled it and is fulfilling it in the true Israel, the church. The kingdom of God was taken from Israel as a nation and given to the true Israel (Matt. 21:43; cf. Luke 12:32). The true Israel was, in Jesus' time, the remnant of faithful believing Jews—the disciples. True Israel now includes believing Gentiles who are being grafted into this body along with faithful Jews (Rom. 11).

If the true Israel, consisting of the faithful Jewish remnant and ingrafted Gentiles, is now fulfilling the promises made to Israel in the Old Testament, then is God through with the Jewish people as a whole forever? That is precisely the question Paul addresses in Romans 9–11. There God teaches that He has not permanently rejected the Jews as a whole (Rom. 11:1). They were hardened in part to bring salvation to the Gentiles (11:7–11). When the fullness of the Gentiles has been grafted into the olive tree (representing God's people), all Israel will be saved. That does not mean they will be brought into Palestine. They will be grafted back into the one good olive tree, the church. There is now no separate purpose for the Jews apart from Jesus Christ (Gal. 3:28).

5. The church age began at Pentecost and will end at the pretribulation rapture.

The truthfulness of this proposition, as with the first, depends upon how the term "church" is defined. Since the church is the body of Christ, and since it is impossible for anyone past, present, or future to be saved apart from union with Christ, Reformed theology defines the church as the believers of all ages—the elect. Scripture teaches us that all who are saved must be "in Christ" (Rom. 8:1; 1 Cor. 15:22; 2 Cor. 5:17; Eph. 2:12, 13). If no one can be saved without being "in Christ," then Old Testament believers must be in Christ. If the body of Christ or the church includes Old Testament believers, then the "church age," strictly speaking, did not begin at Pentecost. The present age could more precisely be called the "new covenant church age," since the church has existed for many ages.

Nothing in this chapter is meant to minimize the differences brought about by Pentecost. As we demonstrated above, one of those differences is the new covenant. We are no longer under the old covenant. We also now have the Holy Spirit, who gives us the power to obey the law of God written upon our hearts. But despite these differences we cannot deny the clear scriptural truth that New Testament saints are heirs together with the saints of the Old Testament. We are one body of believers, the body of Christ.

NOTES

1. Compare also Gen. 22:17 with 1 Kings 4:20.
2. See also Ezek. 36:24–38.
3. J. Dwight Pentecost, *Things to Come* (Grand Rapids: Zondervan, 1958), 116.
4. J. Dwight Pentecost, *Thy Kingdom Come* (Wheaton: Victor Books, 1990), 173.
5. John F. Walvoord, *The Millennial Kingdom* (Grand Rapids: Zondervan, 1959), 209.
6. Pentecost, *Things to Come*, 116.

CHAPTER

5

The Unity of Believers

Five of the seven propositions that form the dispensational doctrine of the church have been examined. Because of the importance of the last two propositions, they will be examined together in this chapter. These two propositions are at the heart of the debate between dispensationalism and nondispensationalism.

6. The church, or body of Christ, consists only of those believers saved between Pentecost and the rapture.

7. The church, or body of Christ, therefore does not include Old Testament believers.

This chapter will attempt to demonstrate the unity of believers of all ages and the essential continuity between true Israel and the church. Our focus will be on some of the scriptural passages that demonstrate most clearly the doctrine that there is one body of believers.[1]

32

Romans 11:11-24

Romans 11:11–24 teaches perhaps as clearly as any passage in the Bible the unity of believers of all ages. To reconcile it with dispensationalism would require doing extreme injustice to this biblical text. The main points of the passage may be summarized as follows:

1. From the context it is clear that the cultivated olive tree is natural Israel (cf. Jer. 11:16; Isa. 17:4–6).
2. The natural branches that are broken off are unbelieving Israelites (Rom. 11:17, 20).
3. The good branches that remain are believing Israelites (vv. 17–18).
4. The wild branches grafted into the good olive tree are believing Gentiles (vv. 17, 19).

Notice that there is only *one* good olive tree. It had been composed of both unbelieving and believing Jews in the Old Testament. But now the bad branches, the unbelieving Jews, have been broken off, leaving only the believing Jews—the true Israel of God—to whom believing Gentiles are now being grafted as to a good tree. And if unbelieving Jews repent and believe, they too are grafted back into the olive tree.

Notice also that God does not plant a brand new tree. He does not break off believing Jews and believing Gentiles from their respective trees and graft them into a third, new tree, all the while maintaining the unbelieving Jewish tree. Yet that is precisely what dispensationalism teaches concerning the relation of Jews and Gentiles to the church. Romans 11 contradicts the heart of the dispensational doctrine of the church.

Ephesians 2:11-19

In Ephesians 2 Paul compares the former state of the Gentiles to their present state. He lists five things that were true of them before they became Christians but now no longer describe them. According to verse 12, the gentile Christians *were*

(1) separate from Christ,
(2) excluded from the commonwealth of Israel,
(3) strangers to the covenants of promise,
(4) without hope,
(5) without God in the world.

These five descriptions stand or fall together. All five *were* true of the Gentiles, and all five are *no longer* true of gentile Christians. We cannot pick and choose which ones apply to gentile believers. Paul applies all of them or none of them. Likewise, all gentile Christians *are now*

(1) in Christ,
(2) included in the commonwealth of Israel,
(3) heirs of the covenants of promise,
(4) with hope,
(5) with God in the world.

Dispensationalists grant that 1, 4, and 5 are true of gentile Christians, but not 2 and 3. Paul, however, argues that *everything* in verse 12 was formerly true of the Gentiles and that *everything* in verse 12 is no longer true of the gentile Christians. If believing Gentiles are no longer separate from Christ, they are also no longer separate from the commonwealth of Israel. If they are now with hope, they are also now heirs of the covenants of promise.

Hebrews 11:39–40

"And all these, having gained approval through their faith, did not receive what was promised, because God had provided something better for us, so that apart from us they should not be made perfect."

These verses occur after the author of Hebrews lists some of the giants of faith in the Old Testament. These Old Testament believers are "made perfect" together *with* us (New Testament believers), not "apart from us." Are we to believe that Abraham, the father of the faithful, will not be part of the body of Christ (the church) simply because he lived prior to the Cross? Certainly not! New Testament believers are coheirs of the promises made to Abraham and to his Seed, Jesus Christ. We are members of the same body of Christ as are Abraham, David, Noah, and *all* the believers of the Old Testament. No man (past, present, or future) can be saved apart from union with Christ.

The Word of God says, "For as in Adam all die, so also in Christ all shall be made alive" (1 Cor. 15:22). All sinners, both before and after Christ, are *in* Adam. And all who are saved, both before and after Christ, are *in* Christ. All men are either dead in Adam, or they are alive in Christ. No one is in neutral.

Revelation 21:9–14

In this passage we see John's vision of the New Jerusalem descending from heaven. The symbolic significance of this text is important for our study. The city is called the bride of the Lamb, and the Lamb is Christ; so the city is the bride of Christ (v. 9). The bride of Christ is a common symbol used to picture the church (John 3:29; Rom. 7:2–4; 2 Cor. 11:2; Eph. 5:25–33; Rev. 19:7–8). If the New Jerusalem is the bride of Christ, and the bride of Christ is the church, then the New Jerusalem is the church.

Several things about the New Jerusalem are relevant to our discussion. Notice especially whom John describes as belonging in the New Jerusalem or the church. In verse 12 we find that the names of the twelve tribes of Israel are written on the twelve gates of the New Jerusalem. In verse 14 the names of the twelve apostles are written on the foundation stones of the New Jerusalem. This is a beautiful symbolic portrait of the unity of the bride of Christ composed of both Old Testament and New Testament believers. The gates with the names of the twelve tribes of Israel written on them represent Old Testament saints. The foundation stones with the names of the twelve apostles written on them represent New Testament saints. Together they are a beautiful city, the bride of the Lamb, the church of Christ.

Galatians 3:16, 29

"Now the promises were spoken to Abraham and to his seed. He does not say, 'And to seeds,' as referring to many, but rather to one, 'And to your seed,' that is Christ" (v. 16). "And if you belong to Christ, then you are Abraham's seed, heirs according to promise" (v. 29).

We learn from these verses that:

1. The Abrahamic promises were made to Abraham *and* to his seed (v. 16).
2. His Seed is Christ (v. 16).
3. *And* his seed is all who belong to Christ (v. 29).
4. Therefore, the Abrahamic promises belong to Christ *and* to all who are His (v. 29).

The Abrahamic promises belong to all who are in Christ. This includes believers of this present age and believers of previous ages. Again, Scripture demonstrates that all believers must be in one body, the body of Christ. Apart from union with Christ, even the greatest Israelite could not inherit the promises.

The concept of the seed of Abraham cannot be limited merely to physical Jews. It is both a narrower and a broader concept. It is narrower in the sense that it truly applies to only one literal Jew, the Lord Jesus Christ. It is broader in the sense that it also applies to all, whether Jew or Gentile, who believe in Jesus and are united with Him.

The dispensational claim that the body of Christ consists only of believers in this age, and that Old Testament believers are not part of the body of Christ, does not stand the test of Scripture. As we have seen, all who are saved are in Christ, and all who are not saved are in Adam. All who are saved are in the one good olive tree. All who are saved are the seed of Abraham because they are all in Christ. All who are saved are coheirs of the promises and are included in the commonwealth of Israel.

No one is saved who is not a part of the body of Christ. The dispensational doctrine of two separate bodies of believers is biblically indefensible. Nowhere does the Bible support the view that some are saved apart from the body of Christ. Jesus Christ is the head of one body of believers, which includes every believer since Adam. When He comes again, His church will be complete, and every believer who has ever lived will be there to rejoice and glorify God. The last believer to be saved in this age will sit down with Noah and Abraham and David, as well as with Peter and John and Paul. We will all be together as *one* with our Lord forever.

NOTES

1. I am indebted to William E. Bell's dissertation, "A Critical Evaluation of the Pre-Tribulation Rapture Doctrine in Christian Eschatology" (Ph.D. diss., New York University, 1967), for many of the ideas in this chapter.

6

The Scriptural Doctrine of Israel and the Church

Having examined Scripture, we have found the dispensational doctrine of the church to be biblically indefensible. The people of God of all ages are one body—the body of Christ—and the body of Christ is the church. The purpose of this chapter is to clarify the scriptural doctrine of the relationship between Israel and the church.

We must first note that if "Israel" is defined as natural, national, or unbelieving Israel, then obviously "Israel" is not the church. The political, ethnic nation of Israel is no more equivalent to the church than any other nation is. Reformed theology does not teach that the church is equivalent to the nation of Israel as a political entity.

The relationship that does exist between Old Testament national Israel and the New Testament visible church is "typical," meaning that Israel was a "type" or foreshadow of the church to come. The nation of Israel included both believers and unbelievers. The visible church (those who have made a verbal profession of faith) also includes both believers and unbelievers. The relationship between Old Testament national Israel and the New Testament visible, professing church is not a relationship of equivalence but of type and antitype, or shadow and reality.

If, however, we define "Israel" as true Israel or Old Testament believers, we discover a different relationship. There is an organic, living relationship between Old Testament believers and New Testament believers. They are one body joined together under one head, the Lord Jesus Christ.

During most of the Old Testament era there were essentially three groups of people: the gentile nations, national Israel, and true Israel. True Israel is often mentioned in the Old Testament as the remnant (Isa. 10:21–22). Though the nation of Israel was often involved in idolatry, apostasy, and rebellion, God always kept for Himself a remnant who trusted in Him and who would not bow the knee to Baal (1 Kings 19:18). Hebrews 11 lists a number of those who were among true Israel. Even in the Old Testament era, not all were Israel who descended from Israel (Rom. 9:6). True Israel included men and women such as Abraham and Isaac and Jacob, Sarah and Deborah and Hannah, David and Joash, Isaiah and Daniel. Of those born physical Israelites, only the believers were true Israel (see figure 1).

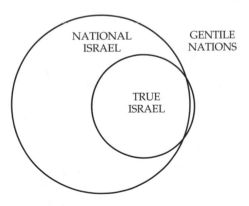

Figure 1. The Old Testament.

When Jesus was born, the faithful remnant of true Israel included believers such as Simeon and Anna (Luke 2:25–38). During Jesus' adult ministry the true Israel was most visible in His true disciples, who believed in Jesus the Messiah. Those who did not believe in Jesus were not true Israel, regardless of their race. That included many of the scribes and Pharisees, who hated Jesus. Though they were physical Jews, they were *not* true Israel (Rom. 2:28–29).

On the Day of Pentecost the true Israel was formed by the Holy Spirit into the nucleus of the new covenant church (Acts 2). The disciples, true Israel, were filled with the Holy Spirit as the prophets had foretold. On this Day of Pentecost it became apparent that true Israel was and is identical to the true church. True Israel had always been the true church, but never before was that connection so clearly seen. The faithful remnant of old Israel became the nucleus of the new Israel. The bad branches (unbelieving Israelites) on the olive tree were at that time cut off by God (Rom. 11:17–24). What remained was true Israel.

Soon afterward, however, an amazing thing began to occur. Believing Samaritans (Acts 8:14–17) and believing Gentiles (Acts 10) began to be grafted into this very same good olive tree, the new Israel of God—the Christian church (see figure 2).

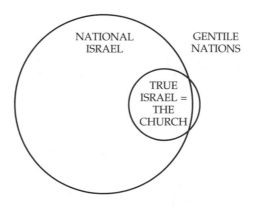

Figure 2. The Day of Pentecost.

The Bible introduces a new name for this new community of believers—"the church." The newness of the church lies in the fact that now believing Jews and believing Gentiles are on equal ground. The church existed in the Old Testament, but only in seed form as the true Israel. That seed grew and finally blossomed on the Day of Pentecost, when the Holy Spirit was poured out and the new covenant was inaugurated.

Since Pentecost more and more gentile believers have been grafted into true Israel, the church (Rom. 11). Now all who are in the church, in Christ, are coheirs of the covenants and promises regardless of their race (Eph. 2:12–13). That is why in one sense Israel is distinct from the church, and in another sense it is identical. The church—true Israel—was, is, and always will be distinct from the Christ-rejecting nation of Israel in the same way that it is distinct from Christ-rejecting gentile nations (see figure 3).

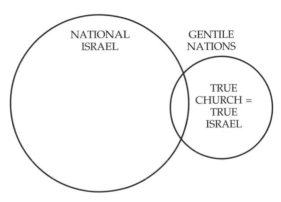

Figure 3. The Present Age.

But Old Testament believers, true Israel, are *not* distinct from New Testament believers. A true Israel always existed within the nation of Israel. Most of these Old Testament believers lived and died before the Messiah came. Some lived to see His day, and they rejoiced. By the Day of Pentecost, *all* who had ever been part of the true Israel, whether dead like Moses or alive like Peter, were united to the risen Christ. Since that day every believer, whether Jew or Gentile, has been united to this *one* good tree. We cannot say that true Israel ceased to be true Israel simply because God has decided to ingraft believing Gentiles. God could have raised up children of Abraham from stones if He wished (Matt. 3:9). Instead, He decided to raise up children of Abraham from Gentiles. The true Israel was and is the true church, and the true church is the true Israel.

That is what Scripture teaches us concerning the relationship between Israel and the church. The foundational doctrine of dispensationalism is unbiblical. As Christians, we have no choice but to reject it and affirm the oneness of the true Israel and the true church.

PART 3

The Dispensational Doctrine of Salvation

CHAPTER

7

The Sinfulness of Sin

The dispensational doctrine of salvation is not unique. What is distinctive about dispensationalism, as we have seen, is its doctrine of the church. Its doctrine of salvation is shared by many nondispensationalists. Why, then, should we examine this doctrine if it is not a distinctive of dispensationalism? There are several important reasons.

First, dispensationalism claims to be a "moderate" variety of Calvinism.[1] Therefore, we need to examine and compare dispensationalism and Calvinism to determine whether that claim is true. Second, because the dispensational doctrine of salvation is taught by the majority of evangelical Christians in the United States and around the world, it is a doctrine of great practical consequence. Third, since the truth of all of God's Word is interrelated, major errors in one teaching often have profound effects on our understanding of other doctrines.

Professing to be "moderate" Calvinists, dispensationalists often claim to teach four of the "five points of Calvinism." Those five points have traditionally been identified by the acronym TULIP:

T   Total Depravity
U   Unconditional Election
L   Limited Atonement
I   Irresistible Grace
P   Perseverance of the Saints

Do dispensationalists subscribe to all but one of these five points as they claim to? In order to answer that question, we will examine those five doctrines in this and the following chapters, comparing the five points of Calvinism with the dispensational doctrines of salvation. Most importantly, we will evaluate each position in the light of Scripture.

Do Dispensationalists Believe in Total Depravity?

This chapter will focus on the first of the five points, namely "total depravity." But first we need to take a brief look at the historical background to the five points of Calvinism.

In 1610, the Arminians (followers of James Arminius) in the Netherlands wrote a document containing five articles. The document was called the "Remonstrance," a word that means "protest," because it took issue with a number of key teachings of the Reformed churches. In response, a synod (church assembly) was called to meet in the city of Dort in 1618 for the purpose of examining the Arminian doctrines. After thorough study, the five Arminian doctrines were condemned, and documents that expressed the Calvinist responses were written and adopted. These five responses composed by the Synod of Dort have in time become known as the five points of Calvinism.

The Canons of Dort express the first of the five points of Calvinism, total depravity, this way:

> Therefore, all people are conceived in sin and are born children of wrath, unfit for any saving good, inclined

to evil, dead in their sins, and slaves to sin; without the grace of the regenerating Holy Spirit they are neither willing nor able to return to God, to reform their distorted nature, or even to dispose themselves to such reform. (Article 3, Third Main Point)

Notice especially that in the Calvinist doctrine of total depravity, the sinner is spiritually dead. He is not merely sick or disabled; he is dead. Sin has affected every part of his being.

Pelagianism (a fifth-century forerunner to Arminianism) taught that man is born good, without sin. He has the free will to choose whether or not to sin, and it is actually possible to live a sinless life. Semi-Pelagianism teaches that although man is not born good, neither is he born totally depraved. He is born with the sickness of sin, which must be cured. Man has the ability to do many good things, including the ability to seek the cure for his disease from God. It is as if God has prepared a vaccine to treat the disease of sin, and He offers it to all men. The vaccine can only be applied, however, if man asks for it. In other words, man's salvation ultimately rests upon his own free choice. Salvation depends upon man.

The doctrine that Calvin taught was vigorously defended by Augustine against Pelagius during the fifth century. In that view man is not born well, nor is he born sick. He is in fact spiritually stillborn—dead. People are incapable of doing anything truly good in the sight of God. They are even incapable of *wanting* to do anything good. The Calvinist doctrine is well summarized by David Steele and Curtis Thomas:

> Because of the fall, man is unable of himself to savingly believe the gospel. The sinner is dead, blind, and deaf to the things of God; his heart is deceitful and desperately corrupt. His will is not free, it is in bondage to his evil nature, therefore, he will not—indeed he cannot—choose good over evil in the spiritual realm. Consequently, it takes much more than the Spirit's assistance to bring a sinner to Christ—it takes regeneration by

which the Spirit makes the sinner alive and gives him
a new nature. Faith is not something man contributes
to salvation but is itself a part of God's gift of salvation—it is God's gift to the sinner, not the sinner's gift
to God.[2]

The Arminian doctrine of depravity is essentially semi-
Pelagianism. It may be summarized as follows:

Man's depravity, as a result of the Fall, is not total but
partial. Man has not lost the faculty of self-determination,
nor the ability to freely will that which is good in the
sight of God. Man is the author of Repentance and Faith
unto salvation since the human will is viewed by the
Arminian as one of the causes of Regeneration, if man
freely wills to cooperate with the Holy Spirit.[3]

The question we are asking thus far is not, Which of these
two positions is biblical? but Which one do dispensationalists
believe? Although dispensationalists claim to teach the Calvinistic doctrine of total depravity, they in fact advocate the semi-
Pelagian or Arminian position.

For example, dispensationalism agrees with the Arminian
view that regeneration depends upon man's faith. As Charles
Ryrie, a former professor of theology at Dallas Theological Seminary, writes concerning the relationship between faith and regeneration, "Faith is not the means of regeneration, though it is
the human requirement which when met enables the Spirit to
bring about the new birth."[4] Notice that faith is the sinner's part
in salvation, his "requirement," rather than the gift of the sovereign Lord. The sinner is only crippled; he is not dead in sin. In
fact, Ryrie says that it is the Holy Spirit who needs help, not
man. The Holy Spirit needs man to "enable" Him to give new
life. Man's faith becomes the basis for regeneration. This is
Arminianism.

This, then, is the question: Does man's faith depend upon
regeneration (Calvinism) or does regeneration depend upon

man's faith (Arminianism)? To ask the question another way, Can a dead man believe? Dispensationalists teach the Arminian doctrine that regeneration depends upon man's faith. According to Chafer and Walvoord, regeneration "is entirely a supernatural act of God in response to the faith of man."[5] Basing regeneration on faith, however, contradicts the doctrine of total depravity. The Synod of Dort recognized that if regeneration is in response to faith, then the sinner is not totally depraved; he is not dead to spiritual things. He is able *of himself* to exercise saving faith. All he needs is assistance from the Holy Spirit.

The dispensational doctrine of depravity is not the total depravity taught of old. Nor is it new. It has been advanced before—by the semi-Pelagians in the time of Augustine and by the Arminians since the early seventeenth century. The dispensationalists' claim to be Calvinistic is misleading in the light of history and the clear teachings of the Reformed creeds.

Is the Dispensational View of Depravity Biblical?

Though the dispensational notion of depravity is not Calvinistic, that does not prove it to be untrue. We must turn to Scripture, not Augustine or Calvin, to verify the truthfulness of a doctrine.

Scripture does not paint a very complimentary picture of fallen man. The Bible teaches us clearly that all people are born in sin (Pss. 51:5; 58:3), that they are spiritually dead (Gen. 2:16–17; Rom. 5:12; Eph. 2:1–3; Col. 2:13), and that they must be born again (John 3:5–7). The Bible tells us repeatedly that sinners' hearts are utterly wicked and that they are totally blind to spiritual things (Gen. 6:5; 8:21; Eccl. 9:3; Jer. 17:9; Mark 7:21–23; John 3:19; Rom. 8:7–8; 1 Cor. 2:14; Eph. 4:17–19; 5:8; Titus 1:15).

The pointedness of the biblical passages is striking, as this small sampling indicates:

• Psalm 58:3: "The wicked are estranged from the womb; These who speak lies go astray from birth."

- Epheshians 2:1: "And you were dead in your trespasses and sins."
- Romans 8:7–8: "The mind set on the flesh is hostile toward God; for it does not subject itself to the law of God, for it is *not even able* to do so; and those who are in the flesh *cannot* please God."

The Bible also teaches that sinners are slaves of sin and children of the Devil (John 8:34, 44; Rom. 6:20; Eph. 2:1–2; 2 Tim. 2:25–26; Titus 3:3; 1 John 3:10; 5:19). No one is excluded from this assessment (1 Kings 8:46; 2 Chron. 6:36; Job 15:14–16; Pss. 130:3; 143:2; Prov. 20:9; Eccl. 7:20, 29; Isa. 53:6; 64:6; Rom. 3:9–12, 23; James 3:2, 8; 1 John 1:8, 10). The Bible teaches us that lost sinners are unable either to repent or to believe, and that faith therefore must be the gift of God (Job 14:4; Jer. 13:23; Matt. 7:16–18; 12:33; John 6:44, 65; Rom. 11:35; 1 Cor. 2:14; 4:7; 2 Cor. 3:5; Eph. 2:8).

Again, the biblical assessment of human sinfulness is emphatic, as these verses show:

- John 8:34: "Jesus answered them, 'Truly, truly, I say to you, everyone who commits sin is the slave of sin.'"
- Psalm 143:2: "And do not enter into judgment with Thy servant, For in Thy sight no man living is righteous."
- Romans 3:10–12: "There is none righteous, not even one; there is none who understands, there is none who seeks for God; all have turned aside, together they have become useless; there is none who does good, there is not even one."

This unflattering picture is one reason why the biblical doctrine of human depravity is unpopular. Man, because of his sinful pride, hates being told the hard truth about himself. And the temptation is to seek a softer alternative that appeals to human pride. Dispensationalism has adopted a semi-Pelagian, Arminian doctrine not based on Scripture and has rejected the Calvinistic doctrine of total depravity rooted deeply in Scripture. But the relevant question is not whether we *like* what the Bible teaches. It is whether we will believe God's Word. God has given us His assessment of fallen humanity. We ignore it at great peril.

NOTES

1. See Lewis Sperry Chafer, *Systematic Theology*, 8 vols. (Dallas: Dallas Seminary Press, 1947), 3:184–88; and Robert P. Lightner, *Evangelical Theology: A Survey and Review* (Grand Rapids: Baker, 1986), 59.
2. David N. Steele and Curtis C. Thomas, *The Five Points of Calvinism* (Phillipsburg, N.J.: Presbyterian and Reformed, 1963), 16. The will is free to choose that which it desires, but because of original sin, the desires are only wicked.
3. Duane E. Spencer, *TULIP: The Five Points of Calvinism in the Light of Scripture* (Grand Rapids: Baker, 1979), 66. For an explanation of the freedom of the will and its relation to total depravity see R. C. Sproul, *Chosen by God* (Wheaton: Tyndale House, 1986).
4. Charles Ryrie, *The Holy Spirit* (Chicago: Moody Press, 1965), 64.
5. Lewis Sperry Chafer and John F. Walvoord, *Major Bible Themes*, rev. ed. (Grand Rapids: Zondervan, 1974), 99.

CHAPTER
8

The Sovereign Choice of God

The doctrine of election is considered by many to be the heart of Calvinism. Election is an important doctrine in any system of theology that seeks to be faithful to God's inerrant Word. Recognizing that fact, dispensationalists profess to teach the Calvinistic doctrine of unconditional election. But do they teach the Calvinistic view? Before answering that question, we need to define our terms.

The Calvinistic doctrine of unconditional election may be summarized as follows:

> God's choice of certain individuals unto salvation before the foundation of the world rested solely in His own sovereign will. His choice of particular sinners was not based on any foreseen response or obedience on their part, such as faith, repentance, etc. On the

contrary, God gives faith and repentance to each individual whom He selected. These acts are the result, not the cause of God's choice. Election therefore was not determined by or conditioned upon any virtuous quality or act foreseen in man. Those whom God sovereignly elected He brings through the power of the Spirit to a willing acceptance of Christ. Thus God's choice of the sinner, not the sinner's choice of Christ, is the ultimate cause of salvation.[1]

We need to emphasize two important points in connection with the doctrine of election. First, election in no way makes God arbitrary or unfair. God had every right to leave the entire human race in sin and under condemnation as He has done with the fallen angels. Rather than asking arrogantly, "Why did God only elect some?," we should ask in thankful awe, "Why did God elect any at all?"

One reason Christians have problems with election is that they do not understand the gravity of human sin. They do not understand total depravity. God was not, as it were, looking at a mass of good people and arbitrarily picking and choosing which ones He would save and which ones He would condemn. Instead, He was in a sense looking at a heap of rotting corpses and graciously choosing to bring some back to life. Those who are elect are receiving grace and mercy. Those who are not elect receive deserved wrath.

Second, we must emphasize that those who are elect have nothing to boast about. God's election was based upon His own sovereign good will. It was not based upon anything in us, including faith, repentance, or good works. We must always remember who is sovereign. God is sovereign, not man. Human pride cannot stomach this truth. Sinful men, puffed up with pride, will not submit to this scriptural doctrine because it gives them no room to boast. They deny the clear teaching of Scripture and replace it with the man-made Arminian doctrine of conditional election or with a watered-down version of unconditional election.

The Arminian doctrine of conditional election may be stated in this way:

> God's choice of certain individuals unto salvation before the foundation of the world was based upon His foreseeing that they would respond to His call. He selected only those whom He knew would of themselves freely believe the gospel. Election therefore was determined by or conditioned upon what man would do. The faith which God foresaw and upon which He based His choice was not given to the sinner by God (it was not created by the regenerating power of the Holy Spirit) but resulted solely from man's will. It was left entirely up to man as to who would believe and therefore as to who would be elected unto salvation. God chose those whom He knew would, of their own free will, choose Christ. Thus the sinner's choice of Christ, not God's choice of the sinner is the ultimate cause of salvation.[2]

Dispensationalists teach neither the Calvinistic doctrine of *unconditional* election nor the Arminian doctrine of *conditional* election. They recognize that election is based on neither foreseen merit nor faith.[3] But because of their weak view of depravity and their belief in unlimited atonement, dispensationalists have a confused doctrine of election—an unstable mixture of conditional and unconditional election. As a result, the biblical doctrine is corrupted.

For example, Chafer rightly teaches in some places that *God's election* is the cause of salvation and condemnation.[4] But because of his inadequate doctrine of depravity, he insists elsewhere that both "salvation and condemnation are *conditioned on the individual's reaction* to one and the same thing, namely, the saving grace of God."[5] Here he is proclaiming the Arminian doctrine that salvation is conditioned upon something man does rather than something God does.

The biblical doctrine of election does not give man this

determinative role in the work of salvation. God's election is the ultimate cause of salvation. The effectual substitutionary atonement of Christ is the ground of salvation. The application of salvation is accomplished by the regenerating work of the Holy Spirit in which He graciously gives dead sinners spiritual life. Even faith itself is a gracious gift from God, a part of the regenerating work of the Holy Spirit. Faith is not a "work" of man. It is not man's "part" in accomplishing salvation. In regeneration the Holy Spirit gives new spiritual life to one who is spiritually dead. In doing so, He imparts living faith and true repentance.

Faith may be likened to breathing. At the moment God grants us life, He gives us breath and we breathe. We do not breathe until we are alive and God has breathed into our nostrils the breath of life (Gen. 2:7). Likewise, we do not believe until the Holy Spirit has given us new, spiritual life.

The biblical testimony concerning God's sovereign election is overwhelming. Sinful man rebels against this scriptural doctrine because he is at heart a rebel and hates God's sovereignty. Hatred of this doctrine, however, does not change the fact that it is scriptural and therefore true. God has one elect people, chosen for salvation (Deut. 10:14–15; Pss. 33:12–13; 65:4; 106:5; Hag. 2:23; Matt. 11:27; 22:14; 24:22, 24, 31; Luke 18:7; Rom. 8:28–30, 33; 11:28; Col. 3:12; 1 Thess. 5:9; Titus 1:1; 1 Peter 1:1–2; 2:8–9; Rev. 17:14).

Consider, for example, Paul's words in two passages:

- Romans 8:28–30: "We know that God causes all things to work together for good to those who love God, to those who are called according to His purpose. For whom He foreknew, He also predestined to become conformed to the image of His Son, that He might be the first-born among many brethren; and whom He predestined, these He also called; and whom He called, these He also justified; and whom He justified, these He also glorified."
- Ephesians 1:3–5: "Blessed be the God and Father of our Lord Jesus Christ, who has blessed us with every spiri-

tual blessing in the heavenly places in Christ, just as He chose us in Him before the foundation of the world, that we should be holy and blameless before Him. In love He predestined us to adoption as sons through Jesus Christ to Himself, according to the kind intention of His will."

God's election of some to salvation was not based or conditioned on anything foreseen in man. Faith and repentance are the *fruit* of God's election, not its cause (John 15:16; Acts 13:48; 18:27; Rom. 9:11–13, 16; 10:20; 1 Cor. 1:27–29; Eph. 1:4, 11; 2:10; Phil. 1:29; 2:12–13; 1 Thess. 1:4–5; 2 Thess. 2:13–14; 2 Tim. 1:9; James 2:5; Rev. 13:8; 17:8). Ultimately, election is based upon God's sovereign good pleasure (Ex. 33:19; Deut. 7:6–7; Matt. 20:15; Rom. 9:10–24; 11:4–6, 33–36; Eph. 1:5).

The Word of God is explicit, as the following sample verses show:

- John 15:16: "You did not choose Me, but I chose you, and appointed you, that you should go and bear fruit, and that your fruit should remain, that whatever you ask of the Father in My name, He may give to you."
- Romans 9:11–18: "Though the twins were not yet born, and had not done anything good or bad, in order that God's purpose according to His choice might stand, not because of works, but because of Him who calls, it was said to her, 'The older will serve the younger.' Just as it is written, 'Jacob I loved, but Esau I hated.' What shall we say then? There is no injustice with God, is there? May it never be! For He says to Moses, 'I will have mercy on whom I have mercy, and I will have compassion on whom I have compassion.' So then it does not depend on the man who wills or the man who runs, but on God who has mercy. For the Scripture says to Pharaoh, 'For this very purpose I raised you up, to demonstrate My power in you, and that My name might be proclaimed throughout the whole earth.' So

then He has mercy on whom He desires, and He hardens whom He desires."

- Philippians 1:29: "For to you it has been granted for Christ's sake, not only to believe in Him, but also to suffer for His sake."

Like the doctrine of total depravity, the doctrine of unconditional election is not popular, even among the elect. It makes no appeal to human arrogance, pride, and self-centeredness. It leaves people with no reason to boast of their goodness or faith. It gives no glory to man but instead gives all honor to God.

We were wicked and rebellious sinners deserving of nothing but God's eternal wrath. For His own sake and His own glory God decided before the foundation of the world to save some of us and leave the rest to their deserved punishment. He sent His Son to die for our sins and purchase our redemption. He sent the Holy Spirit into our lives to apply this salvation to us. The Spirit gave us life, faith, and repentance. We have been justified. We are being sanctified. And one day we will be glorified and made perfect. We will forever be with the Lord Jesus Christ, who died and rose from death that we too may live forever. We deserved no part of this. We caused no part of this. We accomplished no part of this. God did it all. The only thing we can do is fall on our knees, giving thanks and praise to Him.

NOTES

1. David N. Steele and Curtis C. Thomas, *The Five Points of Calvinism* (Phillipsburg, N.J.: Presbyterian and Reformed, 1963), 16–17.

2. Ibid.

3. Lewis Sperry Chafer, *Systematic Theology*, 8 vols. (Dallas: Dallas Seminary Press, 1947), 1:245. One prominent exception to this is Henry C. Thiessen, a dispensationalist who does teach conditional election. See, *Introductory Lectures in Systematic Theology* (Grand Rapids: Eerdmans, 1949), 344.

4. Chafer, *Systematic Theology*, 1:245.

5. Ibid., 3:187, emphasis mine.

CHAPTER
9

The Death of Christ

Dispensationalists claim to be moderate or four-point Calvinists. The point of Calvinism that they reject is the doctrine of "limited" or definite atonement. That is not surprising considering that the vast majority of modern evangelicals reject that doctrine. But as we have seen, popularity is not necessarily an accurate gauge of truth—Scripture is. Sadly, most Christians have never actually studied what the Scriptures teach concerning the death of Christ. They have preferred instead to repeat what they have been told by popular preachers and teachers.

The importance of the doctrine of the atonement is obvious. Since it deals directly with the work of Christ and the results of that work, it has enormous significance for sinful men and women. It should be the desire of every serious Christian to study what the Scriptures teach about the atoning work of Christ.

The Calvinistic doctrine of the atonement has traditionally been called "limited atonement." Because of the misunderstanding surrounding the word "limited," some have suggested the use of the words *definite, particular,* or *effectual.* Steele and Thomas provide the following definition of definite atonement:

> Christ's redeeming work was intended to save the elect only and actually secured salvation for them. His death was a substitutionary endurance of the penalty of sin in the place of certain specified sinners. In addition to putting away the sins of His people, Christ's redemption secured everything necessary for their salvation, including faith which unites them to Him. The gift of faith is infallibly applied by the Spirit to all for whom Christ died, thereby guaranteeing their salvation.[1]

The Arminian doctrine is commonly called "unlimited" atonement and may be defined as follows:

> Christ's redeeming work made it possible for everyone to be saved but did not actually secure the salvation of anyone. Although Christ died for all men and for every man, only those who believe in Him are saved. His death enabled God to pardon sinners on the condition that they believe, but it did not actually put away anyone's sins. Christ's redemption becomes effective only if man chooses to accept it.[2]

Since dispensationalism openly espouses the Arminian doctrine of unlimited atonement, this chapter will examine just that doctrine in the light of Scripture.

Who "Limits" the Atonement?

The term "limited" atonement is not particularly helpful because in reality both Calvinism and Arminianism "limit" the atonement. If Christ's death secured salvation as Calvinism teaches, and it was also for every man as Arminianism teaches, then we would have to conclude that all people are saved. But both Calvinists and conservative Arminians deny universal salvation. They both accept the biblical teaching that some people are not saved. And therefore they both see some limitation of what Jesus' atoning work actually accomplished. Either the *extent* of the atonement is limited: Jesus made full atonement for some (Calvinism). Or else the *value* of the atonement is limited: Jesus made potential atonement for all (Arminianism).

The crucial question is this: Did Jesus Christ die to *save* sinners or to make salvation *possible?* The dispensational and Arminian view, as expressed by Robert Lightner, is that Christ died "to *make possible* the salvation of every lost sinner, to make them all savable."[3] Lewis Sperry Chafer likewise contends "that the death of Christ of itself saves no man, either actually or potentially, but that it does render all men savable."[4]

Problems with Unlimited Atonement

There are at least three serious problems with these claims.

Problem 1: What Does Scripture Actually Say? The Bible never says that Jesus died to make people "savable." It clearly and emphatically teaches that Jesus died to *save* sinners (Rom. 5:10; Gal. 3:13). In Matthew 18:11 Jesus declares that "the Son of Man has come to save that which was lost." He died to *save,* not to make salvation possible. If the Arminian and dispensational doctrine were true, we would not have unlimited atonement; we would have "possible" atonement, which is no atonement at all. There are two choices:

1. Jesus saves.
   OR
2. Jesus makes salvation possible.

Scripture teaches the one. Dispensationalism and Arminianism teach the other. And that raises the question, "If

The Death of Christ

Jesus merely makes salvation possible, what makes salvation actual?" The dispensational answer is that a person's faith makes salvation actual.

Problem 2: Is Faith the Decisive Work? Unlimited atonement changes salvation into a cooperative effort between God and man. Jesus did His part on the cross by making us savable. Now we do our part by believing. What makes salvation actual is our faith, rather than the objective work of Jesus Christ applied to us by the Holy Spirit. But that is simply not biblical. It is works salvation! Man is not saved by his own faith. He is saved by God *through* faith, and even that faith is the gift of God (Eph. 2:8). Any doctrine of salvation that teaches that Jesus does His part in salvation and that we do what He left undone is so blatantly unbiblical that it should not need refutation.

The implications of unlimited atonement must be made very clear. If one follows this doctrine to its conclusion, he is left with either universalism or self-salvation. If, on the one hand, Jesus' death actually secured redemption *and* He died for all men, then all men must be redeemed. But every dispensationalist rightly condemns such universalism as heresy. If, on the other hand, Jesus died for all men and all men are *not* saved, then Jesus' death was *not* effectual. He did not actually redeem anyone on the cross. He did not save. In the words of the dispensationalists and Arminians, "He merely made salvation possible." That would mean that *man* must make salvation actual through his own faith. Man must save himself.

The doctrine of unlimited or "possible" atonement is a doctrine of no atonement at all. Either Jesus saves and does all of the work, or the work is left undone and there is no salvation.

Problem 3: For Whom Is Salvation "Possible"? The dispensational-Arminian doctrine of the atonement cannot consistently be applied. Robert Lightner tells us that "in His death Christ was a substitute for every member of Adam's lost race."[5] Is that true? At the time Christ died, many if not most of Adam's lost race were already in hell. The wicked men who perished in the Flood were in hell. The wicked who perished in Sodom and Gomorrah were in hell. So if Jesus died for every member of Adam's lost race, and He died to make all of these men savable, then what about those who were already in hell? They are members of Adam's lost race. Did Jesus die to make them savable?

No, Jesus died to effectually purchase the salvation of God's elect. He died to secure the salvation of Moses and David and Elijah. He did not die for Jezebel and Pharaoh. That is true of those who lived before the death of Christ, as well as those who live after the Crucifixion. Jesus died to redeem His elect, not to make possible the redemption of everyone.

Scripture teaches us that some people are "vessels of wrath prepared for destruction" (Rom. 9:22). It teaches us that "the LORD has made everything for its own purpose, Even the wicked for the day of evil" (Prov. 16:4). If God has prepared some people for eternal destruction, then is their salvation possible?

Contrary to the dispensational-Arminian doctrine of "possible atonement," the Scriptures teach that the purpose of Christ's death was to guarantee the full salvation of His people (Matt. 1:21; Luke 19:10; 1 Tim. 1:15; 1 Peter 3:18). This is the heart of the debate. Did Jesus' death actually atone for our sins? Did it secure redemption, propitiation, satisfaction, and reconciliation? Or did it only make these possible?

- Matthew 1:21: "And she will bear a Son; and you shall call His name Jesus, for it is He who will *save* His people from their sins."
- 1 Timothy 1:15: "It is a trustworthy statement, deserving full acceptance, that Christ Jesus came into the world to *save* sinners, among whom I am foremost of all."
- 1 John 4:10: "In this is love, not that we loved God, but that He loved us and sent His Son to be *the propitiation* for our sins."

The Bible tells us that reconciliation, justification, regeneration, redemption, satisfaction, propitiation, and sanctification were secured for everyone for whom Christ died (Rom. 3:24–25; 5:8–10; 1 Cor. 1:30; 2 Cor. 5:18–21; Gal. 3:13; Eph. 2:15–16; 5:25–26; Col. 1:13–14, 20–22; Titus 2:14; 3:5–6; Heb. 2:17; 9:12; 13:12; 1 Peter 2:24; 1 John 4:10). Salvation was objectively secured and paid for by Christ on the cross. At the appointed time, the Holy Spirit applies this salvation subjectively to each person for whom Christ died. God receives all the praise and all the glory because salvation is entirely His work from beginning to end.

- Romans 5:10: "For if while we were enemies, we were reconciled to God through the death of His Son, much more, having been reconciled, we shall be saved by His life."
- Colossians 1:20–22: ". . . and through Him to reconcile all things to Himself, having made peace through the blood of His cross; through Him, I say, whether things on earth or things in heaven. And although you were formerly alienated and hostile in mind, engaged in evil deeds, yet He has now reconciled you in His fleshly body through death, in order to present you before Him holy and blameless and beyond reproach."
- Hebrews 9:12: "And not through the blood of goats and calves, but through His own blood, He entered the holy place once for all, having obtained eternal redemption."
- Revelation 5:9: "And they sang a new song, saying, 'Worthy art Thou to take the book, and to break its seals; for Thou wast slain, and didst purchase for God with Thy blood men from every tribe and tongue and people and nation.'"

Scripture tells us that Jesus' death fulfilled a plan made before the foundation of the world (Rom. 8:30; 9:22–23; Eph. 1:4–6, 9, 11; 1 Thess. 5:9; 2 Tim. 1:9), and His death was intended to infallibly save the elect (Matt. 1:21; 20:28; 26:28; John 10:11;

11:50–53; Acts 20:28; Rom. 8:32–34; Eph. 5:25–27; Heb. 2:17; 9:15, 28; Rev. 5:9). The Word of God is clear. The value of Christ's death cannot be limited. It secured the salvation of those for whom it was accomplished. Jesus' death purchased a perfect salvation for everyone for whom He died. Since all men are not saved, He did not die for all men.

"Problem Passages": Do They Support Unlimited Atonement?

A number of passages are often used to support the claim that Jesus died for every individual who ever lived. In order to understand these passages, several biblical principles must be remembered. Most of the passages that allegedly teach unlimited atonement are explained by one or more of these principles.

1. All Christians acknowledge that since the divine nature of Christ is infinite, the value of His death must therefore be infinite, or sufficient to save all.
2. The dividing wall between Jews and Gentiles has been removed. The kingdom has been enlarged beyond the boundaries of national Israel to include Gentiles (Joel 2:28; Rom. 1:5; Eph. 2:14–17; Col. 3:11). The Jews wrongly believed that salvation was for them alone (Acts 13:45–50; Eph. 3:5–6; 1 Thess. 2:15–16).
3. Indefinite terms such as "all" and "world" usually do not refer to every individual who ever lived, and therefore they must be interpreted in light of their contexts.
4. There is a mixture of the elect and the nonelect throughout the world, a fact that necessitates the universal offer of the gospel.

As we give attention to the specific texts said to teach that Christ died for everyone, we must keep in mind the multitude of clear biblical passages concerning the actual purpose and effects of the Cross. Christ's death was effectual—it redeemed, reconciled, propitiated, and satisfied. It did not merely make these results possible. The salvation of everyone for whom Jesus died was secured, finished on the cross. With this in mind, we can now examine passages alleged to teach unlimited atonement.

Jesus Died for the "World"

First, there are those texts which speak of Christ's having died for the "world" (John 1:9, 29; 3:16–17; 4:42; 6:51; 2 Cor. 5:19; 1 John 2:1–2; 4:14). Three points may be made about these passages.

1. The word "world" in Scripture does not usually mean every individual human being. In fact, many times it *cannot* mean every human being (John 7:7; 12:19; Rom. 1:8; 1 Cor. 4:9; 11:32). For example, John 14:17 teaches us that the world cannot receive the Spirit of truth. Does that mean it is impossible for anyone who has ever lived to receive the Spirit? No, the context determines the meaning.

2. Since Scripture clearly teaches that Christ's death actually secured salvation, then when the Bible speaks of His dying for the "world," it cannot mean every individual who ever lived. It cannot, that is, unless every individual who ever lived were saved.

3. Therefore, "world" may often mean the *sinful* world generally, including those once thought to be excluded from God's grace, Gentiles (e.g., 1 John 2:1–2). It sometimes refers to all who will ever believe, regardless of race (e.g., John 6:51).

Jesus Died for "All"

Second, there are texts that use the word "all" in reference to those for whom Christ died (Rom. 5:18; 1 Cor. 15:22; 2 Cor. 5:14–15; 1 Tim. 2:4–6; Heb. 2:9; 2 Peter 3:9). Several points must also be made about these passages.

1. Like the word "world," the meaning of "all" must be determined by its context. It does not always mean every individual.

2. Sometimes "all" means all of some kinds (Rom. 5:18; 1 Cor. 15:22; Eph. 4:6). For example, when Romans 5:18 speaks of the justification of "all men," does that mean that every individual who ever lived will be justified? No, in this context "all" means all who believe. Likewise, in Romans 11:26, when Paul says that "all Israel will be saved," even dispensationalists grant that he does not mean every individual Israelite.

3. Sometimes the word "all" means some of all kinds (Jer. 31:34, cf. Heb. 8:11; John 12:32). For example, Paul urges in 1 Timothy 2:1 that "prayers, petitions and thanksgivings, be made on behalf of all men." The next verse makes it clear that he does not mean every individual that ever lived, but all kinds of men, especially those in authority.

4. The prophecies of the Old Testament spoke of "all nations," "all flesh," "all people," etc., being converted, without meaning every individual. Is it unreasonable to suppose that the New Testament authors would use this same kind of language when they speak about the fulfillment of these prophecies in Christ?

Did Jesus Die for Some Who Perish?

Third are those texts which allegedly teach that Christ died for some who will ultimately perish. Two such passages, Romans 14:15 and 1 Corinthians 8:11, simply teach the danger of doing what could lead a weaker brother into sin. A more difficult passage, Hebrews 10:26–29, has at least three possible interpretations.

1. Those who "trample under foot the Son of God" (v. 29) after "receiving a knowledge of the truth" (v. 26) and being "sanctified" (v. 29) are like those in the parable of the sower who spring up temporarily but later fall away or prove unfruitful (Matt. 13:20–22). They are in the covenant community externally and profess faith for a time, but their apostasy proves that their faith was false.

2. Some suggest that the word "he" in the phrase "by which he was sanctified" refers to Christ Himself, and not an

apostate man (cf. John 17:19). In that case, the person renouncing the Son and the Spirit never was "sanctified" and never was the object of Christ's death.

3. Some suggest that this apostasy is merely a hypothetical situation, not a real possibility. The passage does not say that any for whom Jesus died will actually fall away.

Another passage, 2 Peter 2:1, also has several possible interpretations.

1. The false teachers who deny the Master were "bought" or redeemed only in outward appearance.

2. Their redemption is their own false opinion about themselves.

3. They are said to be redeemed because of the judgment of charity. All who profess to partake of redemption must be given the benefit of the doubt until and unless they demonstrate that their profession is false. Only God can judge the heart.

4. Peter is possibly alluding to Deuteronomy 32:6, in which Moses denounces rebellious Jews who were "bought" by God in the Exodus. Because they were "bought" by God, the Jews as a whole belong to God. In this case, Peter is referring to Jewish false teachers of his day, who like the Jewish false teachers of Moses' day, deny the God who "bought" them.

If clear Scriptures are allowed to take precedence over obscure passages, the Arminian position has no foundation. Scripture clearly teaches the efficacy of Christ's death. He died to save men, not to make salvation possible. The so-called problem passages are not really a problem if they are read within the context of the entire Bible. The overwhelming testimony of Scripture is that the purpose of Jesus' death on the cross was to secure the salvation of His people. He accomplished His purpose. It is finished.

NOTES

1. David N. Steele and Curtis C. Thomas, *The Five Points of Calvinism* (Phillipsburg, N.J.: Presbyterian and Reformed, 1963), 17.

2. Ibid.

3. Robert P. Lightner, *The Death Christ Died: A Case for Unlimited Atonement* (Des Plaines, Ill.: Regular Baptist Press, 1967), 67, his emphasis.
4. Lewis Sperry Chafer, *Systematic Theology*, 8 vols. (Dallas: Dallas Seminary Press, 1947), 3:185.
5. Robert P. Lightner, *Evangelical Theology: A Survey and Review* (Grand Rapids: Baker, 1990), 209.

CHAPTER 10

The Irresistible Power
of the Spirit

Thus far we have seen that dispensationalists profess to believe in the Calvinistic doctrines of total depravity and unconditional election, but not limited or definite atonement. Dispensationalists also claim to teach the doctrine of irresistible grace. Before we examine that claim, we need to define the issue. The Calvinist doctrine of irresistible grace may be stated as follows:

> In addition to the outward general call to salvation which is made to everyone who hears the gospel, the Holy Spirit extends to the elect a special inward call that inevitably brings them to salvation. The external call (which is made to all without distinction) can be, and often is, rejected; whereas the internal call (which is made only to the elect) cannot be rejected; it always results in conversion. By means of this special call the

Spirit irresistibly draws sinners to Christ. He is not limited in His work of applying salvation by man's will, nor is He dependent upon man's cooperation for success. The Spirit graciously causes the elect sinner to cooperate, to believe, to repent, to come freely and willingly to Christ. God's grace, therefore is invincible; it never fails to result in the salvation of those to whom it is extended.[1]

The Westminster Confession of Faith summarizes the doctrine this way in chapter 10, paragraph 1:

All those whom God hath predestinated unto life, and those only, he is pleased, in his appointed and accepted time, effectually to call, by his Word and Spirit, out of that state of sin and death, in which they are by nature, to grace and salvation, by Jesus Christ; enlightening their minds spiritually and savingly to understand the things of God, taking away their heart of stone, and giving unto them a heart of flesh; renewing their wills, and, by his almighty power, determining them to that which is good, and effectually drawing them to Jesus Christ: yet so, as they come most freely, being made willing by his grace.

In contrast to this, the Arminian doctrine of resistible grace may be summarized as follows:

The Spirit calls inwardly all those who are called outwardly by the gospel invitation; He does all that He can to bring every sinner to salvation. But inasmuch as man is free, he can successfully resist the Spirit's call. The Spirit cannot regenerate the sinner until he believes; faith (which is man's contribution) precedes and makes possible the new birth. Thus, man's free will limits the Spirit in the application of Christ's saving work. The Holy Spirit can only draw to Christ those who allow Him to have His way with them. Until the sinner responds, the Spirit cannot give life. God's grace, therefore, is not invincible; it can be, and often is, resisted and thwarted by man.[2]

Do dispensationalists uphold the Calvinistic doctrine of irresistible grace? To answer that, consider first of all that the dispensational doctrine of unlimited atonement destroys the notion of irresistible grace. If Jesus graciously died for all men and some remain lost, then those who are lost resist God's grace. Second, the dispensational doctrine of regeneration conflicts with irresistible grace. If the Holy Spirit's work of regeneration depends upon man's faith, as dispensationalists maintain, then man limits the sovereign work of the Spirit. This essentially Arminian view—that regeneration is based upon and follows faith—replaces irresistible grace with a cooperative effort between man and the Holy Spirit.

Charles Ryrie's words are especially telling in this regard:

> It seems as if grace that is effective would involve no human effort; indeed it would be contrary to human effort. However God has preserved the necessity of believing, and while this is more a human responsibility than a human effort, *it nevertheless is man's part in making efficacious grace effective.*[3]

Note that *man* makes grace effective. Apart from his contribution, efficacious grace is not efficacious. That is a far cry from the doctrine of sovereign irresistible grace. The Arminian, dispensational view reduces efficacious grace to good intentions on God's part. God is left to the mercy of man, not the other way around.

Arminianism is forever seeking to give man a part, however small or large, in the work of salvation. But salvation is God's sovereign work from beginning to end (Rom. 8:29–30). Man cannot and does not contribute anything to God's saving work. Salvation is by divine grace alone without *any* mixture of human works.

Men are dead in sin, totally hopeless and helpless. God the Father sovereignly and unconditionally elected a host of people out of sinful, spiritually dead humanity and chose to save them for His own glory. In due time Jesus came to secure, by His substitutionary death on the cross, the salvation of those whom the Father had chosen. Finally, the Holy Spirit sovereignly and irresistibly applies this perfect and complete salvation to each elect sinner at the appointed time. At absolutely no point does human effort or human work play any part in the sovereign accomplishment and application of salvation. God alone in His infinite mercy and grace saves sinners. It is His work, and all glory and praise belong to Him. There is no room for human boasting.

Scripture speaks often of the Holy Spirit's role in salvation (Rom. 8:14; 1 Cor. 2:10–14; 6:11; 12:3; 2 Cor. 3:6, 17–18; 1 Peter 1:2). God regenerates sinners without their help (Deut. 30:6; Ezek. 36:26–27; John 1:12–13; 3:3–8; 5:21; 2 Cor. 5:17–18; Eph. 2:1, 5, 10; Col. 2:13; Titus 3:5; 1 Peter 1:3, 23; 1 John 5:4). The sovereign work of God in regeneration, apart from human initiative, is clearly expressed in the following verses:

- John 1:12–13: "As many as received Him, to them He gave the right to become children of God, even to those who believe in His name, who were *born not of blood, nor of the will of the flesh, nor of the will of man, but of God."*
- John 5:21: "For just as the Father raises the dead and gives them life, even so the Son also *gives life to whom He wishes."*
- Titus 3:5: "He saved us, not on the basis of deeds which we have done in righteousness, but *according to His mercy,* by the washing of regeneration and renewing by the Holy Spirit."

The Word of God teaches us that the Holy Spirit reveals spiritual things (1 Cor. 2:13–14; Eph. 1:17–18) and that faith and repentance are gifts (Acts 5:31; 11:18; 13:48; 16:14; 18:27; Eph.

2:8–9; Phil. 1:29; 2 Tim. 2:25–26) coming from regeneration. The following are just a few of many passages that convey these truths:

- Acts 16:14: "The Lord opened [Lydia's] heart to respond to the things spoken by Paul."
- 1 Corinthians 2:12–14: "Now we have received, not the spirit of the world, but the Spirit who is from God, that we might know the things freely given to us by God, which things we also speak, not in words taught by human wisdom, but in those taught by the Spirit, combining spiritual thoughts with spiritual words. But a natural man does not accept the things of the Spirit of God; for they are foolishness to him, and he cannot understand them, because they are spiritually appraised."
- Ephesians 2:8–9: "For by grace you have been saved through faith; and that not of yourselves, it is the gift of God; not as a result of works, that no one should boast."
- Philippians 1:29: "For to you it has been granted for Christ's sake, not only to believe in Him, but also to suffer for His sake."

Scripture also teaches that the outward call, the free offer of the gospel, is made to all people. But the irresistible inward call is to the elect only (John 10:26–28; Rom. 1:6–7; 8:30; 9:23–24; 1 Cor. 1:1–2, 9, 23–31; Gal. 1:15–16; Eph. 4:4; 2 Tim. 1:9; Heb. 9:15, 1 Peter 1:15; 2:9; 5:10; 2 Peter 1:3; Jude 1; Rev. 17:14). The application of salvation is all of grace, accomplished solely by God (Isa. 55:11; John 3:27; 17:2; Rom. 9:16; 1 Cor. 3:6–7; 4:7; Phil. 2:12–13; James 1:18; 1 John 5:20). It is God who enables people to respond to the outward call.

- John 3:27: "A man can receive nothing, unless it has been given him from heaven."
- John 6:44: "No one can come to Me, unless the Father who sent Me draws him; and I will raise him up on the last day."

- John 10:26–27: "But you do not believe, because you are not of My sheep. My sheep hear My voice, and I know them, and they follow Me."

The Father elected a multitude before the foundation of the world to be saved. The Son died to secure the salvation of those who had been chosen for eternal life. The Holy Spirit irresistibly and infallibly applies this salvation to each and every one of the elect. That is the scriptural doctrine of salvation. God alone accomplishes everything. Man is simply the recipient of this wonderful grace of God. "For from Him and through Him and to Him are all things. To Him be the glory forever" (Rom. 11:36).

NOTES

1. David N. Steele and Curtis C. Thomas, *The Five Points of Calvinism* (Phillipsburg, N.J.: Presbyterian and Reformed, 1963), 18.
2. Ibid.
3. Charles C. Ryrie, *The Holy Spirit* (Chicago: Moody Press, 1965), 62, emphasis mine.

CHAPTER 11

The Perseverance of the Saints

Dispensationalists and Calvinists agree that a true believer in Christ will never lose his or her salvation. But is the modern evangelical doctrine of "eternal security," which dispensationalists teach, the same thing as the Calvinistic doctrine of the perseverance of the saints?

Calvinism holds that "all who were chosen by God, redeemed by Christ, and given faith by the Spirit are eternally saved. They are kept in faith by the power of almighty God and thus persevere to the end."[1] The traditional Arminian doctrine is that "those who believe and are truly saved can lose their salvation by failing to keep up their faith . . . ."[2] The dispensationalist position, eternal security, is neither Calvinistic nor Arminian.

Eternal security is the view that the new life, given by the Holy Spirit in regeneration, may or may not be lived out by the

Christian and that the security of his salvation is in no way affected by his failure to live a new life. "In other words," John Gerstner explains, "a true believer may not persevere in holiness. Reformed theology teaches that such a failure would prove that the person is not a true believer at all and that only those who persevere to the end will be saved."[3]

According to the dispensational doctrine of eternal security, once a person "believes," nothing he does—even persistent unconfessed sin—can affect his eternal salvation. This, however, differs from the doctrine of the perseverance of the saints. The Reformed doctrine of perseverance says that all who were chosen, redeemed, and regenerated by God are eternally saved and are kept in faith by the power of God. They must and will, therefore, persevere in holiness to the end.

The dispensational view is not that believers *must* but that they *may* persevere in holiness to the end. In fact, according to some dispensationalists, not only is perseverance in holiness unnecessary, but even remaining a believer is unnecessary. Charles Ryrie, for example, argues that a true believer in Christ can become a nonbeliever and yet still be saved. Commenting on a statement by Charles Ellicot, Ryrie argues: "Normally one who has believed can be described as a believer; that is, one who continues to believe. But . . . apparently a believer may come to the place of not believing, and yet God will not disown him, since He cannot disown Himself."[4] Ryrie adds, "Today proponents of lordship/discipleship/mastery salvation . . . conclude that if someone does not continue to believe, then he or she was never a believer in the first place."[5] Ryrie seems to say that a person can be a nonbelieving believer. It is astounding that any Christian would even entertain such an unbiblical idea, much less promote it as truth.

This dispensational doctrine is in direct conflict with Scripture. The apostle John wrote, "They went out from us, but they were not really of us; for if they had been of us, they would have remained with us; but they went out, in order that it might be shown that they all are not of us" (1 John 2:19). Those who renounce Christ, whether they once professed faith or not, are *not* saved. All who claim to be believers and then later renounce Christ and become nonbelievers never were believers in the first place.

The same is true of those who show no fruit of the Spirit and no desire to stop sinning. The apostle Paul explained to Titus, "They profess to know God, but by their deeds they deny Him, being detestable and disobedient, and worthless for any good deed" (Titus 1:16). A past profession of faith does not change the fact that their actions demonstrate their profession to be false. Those who are living in sin and unrepentance must not be given false hope based upon a profession they made in the past. Satan laughs when unbelievers are convinced that they are saved.

Faith is not a one-time event. It is not like signing a contract or an insurance policy. True living faith is a gift from God that begins at a person's new birth and never ends. It is like breathing. As our physical breath results from our physical birth, so our spiritual breath (faith) results from our spiritual birth (regeneration). But our physical breathing does not stop there. Likewise, true living faith begins at a moment in time and then continues. At some stages in the true Christian's life, faith may be very weak, but if it is true faith it will never die. The true believer must and will, by the grace of God, persevere until the end.

Scripture attests to this truth in many places (a mere fraction of which are Isa. 43:1–3; 54:10; Jer. 32:40; Matt. 18:12–14; John 3:16, 36; 5:24; 6:35–40, 47; 10:27–30; 17:11–12, 15; Rom. 5:8–10; 8:1, 29–30, 35–39; 1 Cor. 1:7–9; 10:13; 2 Cor. 4:14, 17; Eph. 1:5, 13–14; 4:30; Col. 3:3–4; 1 Thess. 5:23–24; 2 Tim. 4:18; Heb. 9:12, 15; 10:14; 12:28; 1 Peter 1:3–5; 1 John 2:19, 25; 5:4, 11–13, 20; Jude 1, 24–25). Consider the words of a few sample verses:

- Romans 8:35–39: "Who shall separate us from the love of Christ? Shall tribulation, or distress, or persecution, or famine, or nakedness, or peril, or sword? Just as it is written, 'For Thy sake we are being put to death all day long; we were considered as sheep to be slaughtered.' But in all these things we overwhelmingly conquer through Him who loved us. For I am convinced that neither death, nor life, nor angels, nor principalities, nor things present, nor things to come, nor powers, nor height, nor depth, nor any other created thing, shall be able to separate us from the love of God, which is in Christ Jesus our Lord."

- John 6:37, 39: "All that the Father gives Me shall come to Me, and the one who comes to Me I will certainly not cast out. . . . And this is the will of Him who sent Me, that of all that He has given Me I lose nothing, but raise it up on the last day."
- John 10: 27–29: "My sheep hear My voice, and I know them, and they follow Me; and I give eternal life to them and they shall never perish; and no one shall snatch them out of My hand. My Father, who has given them to Me, is greater than all; and no one is able to snatch them out of the Father's hand."

"Moderate Calvinism"?

Dispensationalists' claims to be Calvinistic have been examined and found wanting. The only doctrine on which dispensationalism comes close to Calvinism is the doctrine of unconditional election. Dispensationalism is not "four-point" Calvinism. At most it is one point Calvinistic, three points Arminian, and one point neither.

The doctrines of grace distilled in the five points of Calvinism have been shown to be the consistent testimony of Scripture. Ultimately Arminianism finds its support not in Scripture but in the pride of sinful men by teaching that a person plays the decisive part in his own salvation.

Arminianism begins by denying that people are totally depraved. Each individual has the power to do some good, at least the ability to exercise saving faith. Man is not dead in sin or utterly hopeless; he is merely sick. God's sovereign election of sinners is based not on His good pleasure but on a person's foreseen faith. An act of man determines what God does in election. Jesus' humiliating and excruciating death on the cross did not save anyone. He was just doing His part to make people savable. Now they must do the decisive part by believing. Christ's work did not completely save. The implication is that Jesus was wrong when he cried out, "It is finished!" It is not finished until man believes.

Arminianism also teaches that man's faith determines whom the Holy Spirit will regenerate. It even suggests that man can remove himself from the almighty hand of God. From beginning to end, Arminianism exalts the power of man and insults the living God. To the extent that a person adopts this man-centered system of ideas, he too is guilty of dishonoring the sovereign God.

Scripture is abundantly clear: those whom the Father chose, and the Son died for, and the Holy Spirit regenerated, will persevere in holiness and faith until the end and will surely be saved for all eternity. For this we can only fall on our knees and thank God. We have nothing to boast about, except to boast in the Lord. Salvation is entirely by grace. It is God's work and His work alone.

NOTES

1. David N. Steele and Curtis C. Thomas, *The Five Points of Calvinism* (Phillipsburg, N.J.: Presbyterian and Reformed, 1963), 18.
2. Ibid.
3. John H. Gerstner, *Wrongly Dividing the Word of Truth* (Brentwood, Tenn.: Wolgemuth & Hyatt, 1991), 142.
4. Charles C. Ryrie, *So Great Salvation* (Wheaton: Victor, 1989), 141.
5. Ibid., 142.

CHAPTER
12

Regeneration

One of the most problematic aspects of the dispensational doctrine of salvation is its view of regeneration. We have noted earlier the problems that result when regeneration is based upon faith. In this chapter we will look more closely at what dispensationalists say about the nature of regeneration.

It may be helpful first to note what the dispensational view of regeneration is not—it is not the Reformed doctrine. Consider, for example the definitions set forth by two leading Reformed theologians. Charles Hodge describes regeneration as the "instantaneous change from spiritual death to spiritual life. Regeneration, therefore, is a spiritual resurrection, the beginning of a new life."[1] According to Louis Berkhof regeneration is "that act of God by which the principle of the new life is implanted in man, and the governing disposition of the soul is made holy."[2]

In Reformed theology, people are spiritually stillborn, born dead in sin. When the Holy Spirit regenerates us, we are "born again." We are resurrected spiritually and become a new creation. This understanding of regeneration is closely connected to the doctrine of total depravity. Regeneration is made necessary by the depth of human sinfulness. If we were not *dead* in sin—but only sick—we would have no need of regeneration, only rehabilitation. But dead people need life, not medicine. And new life is what the Holy Spirit gives us when He regenerates us.

Dispensationalism teaches a radically different doctrine of regeneration. For dispensationalists, regeneration is not the resurrection of the spiritually dead human nature but the addition of a divine nature. John F. Walvoord, for example, tells us that "eternal life involves first of all the creation of a divine nature in the regenerated person."[3] Lewis Sperry Chafer is even more explicit: "As human generation begets a life 'after its kind' so divine regeneration means the impartation of a life from God which is wholly foreign to that of fallen man. It is the divine nature."[4] He adds that "to be born of God means an induction into the order of heavenly beings."[5] And again, "With the reception of the divine nature which is imparted through regeneration, the Christian becomes a complex being, possessing two natures—not, two personalities. . . ."[6]

Problems with the Dispensational View

The dispensational doctrine of regeneration has serious problems. In the first place, it virtually deifies man. The regenerated individual is one person with two natures—one human and one divine. That is to say, the regenerate are God-men. If that is true, Jesus Christ—the divine-human God-man—is not unique.

But Scripture teaches that Jesus Christ is the unique God-man. When human beings are saved, they become new creatures, not divine beings in any sense. God is the Creator, and humanity is His creation. His divine nature is infinite. Our nature is finite. For all eternity God will remain God, and men will remain men.

When someone is regenerated he or she receives eternal

life. But a man remains a man with a human nature only. Though the Holy Spirit indwells him, the Spirit remains distinct from him. We are united with Christ by His Spirit; yet our nature remains human, nothing more. We partake of Christ's life, but this does not change our essence or make us somehow divine. God is God, and man is man. The only one to possess both a divine and a human nature in one person is the God-man Himself, Jesus Christ.

It is therefore important to stress that God does not give us a divine nature when He regenerates us. He gives new life to our spiritually dead human nature. The result is a spiritually alive human nature, but not a divine nature. That cannot be overemphasized. If you have a divine nature, you are God. But remember that the promise "You will be like God" was part of the original lie of Satan (Gen. 3:5). We must fight against any doctrine that teaches that man becomes divine. Christians are not little Gods.

A second and related problem with the dispensational doctrine of regeneration is that it wreaks havoc in the Christian's spiritual life. Believers become confused as to exactly how many entities exist within them. Consider, for example, Robert Lightner's explanation of the Christian's inner struggle with sin.

> The internal conflict manifests itself in everyday life as the believer is tempted to sin. The source of this conflict is the old sin nature, which is the root cause of the deeds of sin. In the conflict the believer is not passive. He has a vital role in determining to whom he will give allegiance—the old sin nature or the new nature.[7]

Within the same person described above, we have not one or even two but at least three distinct entities.

1. The old sin nature—the root cause of all sin.
2. The new divine nature—which is unable to sin.
3. The believer—who chooses which of the other two will be in control.

The dispensational doctrine leaves several questions unanswered: Who is the believer? Is he the old nature? If so, how can he choose to let the new nature have control since the old nature can only do evil? Is he the new nature? If so, why would he ever let the old nature regain control? Is he a combination of the two natures? If so, why is he described as if he were a neutral third party choosing between the two natures?

It is unclear how this neutral believer is supposed to choose which nature will be in charge—the old sin nature or the new divine nature. Perhaps he is to ask the indwelling Holy Spirit for help. But if we add the Holy Spirit to this formula, we have four entities in the Christian. The believer suffers from a severe case of spiritual multiple personality disorder. And the more he dwells on these things, the more confused he becomes about who he or she really is.[8]

What Does the Bible Say?

The scriptural doctrine is much simpler to understand. The Holy Spirit sovereignly "brings persons into living union with Christ, changing their hearts so that they who were spiritually dead become spiritually alive, now able and willing to repent of sin, believe the gospel, and serve the Lord."[9] Regeneration need not be a confusing doctrine. The following verses speak clearly of a transformation from spiritual deadness to spiritual life, not the addition of a second nature alongside the old one (see also Deut. 30:6; John 1:12–13; 3:3-8; 1 Peter 1:3–4; 1 John 2:29; 3:9; 4:7; 5:1,4, 18):

- Ezekiel 36:26: "I will give you a new heart and put a new spirit within you; and I will remove the heart of stone from your flesh and give you a heart of flesh."
- John 5:24: "Truly, truly, I say to you, he who hears My word, and believes Him who sent Me, has eternal life, and does not come into judgment, but has passed out of death into life."

- 2 Corinthians 5:17: "Therefore if any man is in Christ, he is a new creature; the old things passed away; behold, new things have come."
- Ephesians 2:4-6: "But God, being rich in mercy, because of His great love with which He loved us, even when we were dead in our transgressions, made us alive together with Christ (by grace you have been saved), and raised us up with Him, and seated us with Him in the heavenly places, in Christ Jesus."

Regeneration is spiritual resurrection. If we are in Christ, we who were once spiritually dead are now spiritually alive because of the work of the Holy Spirit.

NOTES

1. Charles Hodge, *Systematic Theology,* 3 vols. (Grand Rapids: Eerdmans, 1989 [1872]), 3:5.
2. Louis Berkhof, *Systematic Theology* (Grand Rapids: Eerdmans, 1939), 469.
3. John F. Walvoord, *The Holy Spirit* (Grand Rapids: Zondervan, 1954), 135.
4. Lewis Sperry Chafer, *Systematic Theology,* 8 vols. (Dallas: Dallas Seminary Press, 1947), 6:35.
5. Ibid., 6:36.
6. Ibid., 6:184.
7. Robert P. Lightner, *Evangelical Theology: A Survey and Review* (Grand Rapids: Baker, 1990), 206.
8. For a biblical perspective on the spiritual battle waged by every Christian, see R. C. Sproul, *Pleasing God* (Wheaton, Ill.: Tyndale House, 1988).
9. Anthony Hoekema, *Saved by Grace* (Grand Rapids: Eerdmans, 1989), 94.

CHAPTER
13

The Doctrine of the Law

The dispensational doctrine of the law is rooted in its radical distinction between the people of God before Christ and the people of God after Christ. Dispensationalism teaches that the law was given only to the nation of Israel, and that the entire law (including the Ten Commandments) was done away with when Christ came. It therefore has no use in the life of the believer today. Charles Ryrie explains, "The law was never given to Gentiles and is expressly done away for the Christian."[1] This negation of God's law is found throughout the writings of dispensationalists.[2]

In this chapter we shall examine the dispensational doctrine of the law under seven headings.

1. God's Law Expresses His Holy Character

Reformed theology understands the law of God to be an expression of His holy character. John Murray explains that "moral law is the moral perfection of God coming to expression for the regulation of life and conduct."[3] Dispensationalists concur that the law expresses God's character. Lewis Sperry Chafer writes: "The foundation of all divine law is the Person of God. What He requires is only the expression of what He is. Since He is holy, just and good, His ideals, standards and requirements must be holy, just and good."[4]

Chafer's statement is fine as far as it goes. We need to remember, however, that God is not only holy, just, and good but also perfect and unchanging. And if God is perfect and unchanging, His law is also perfect and unchanging (Ps. 19:7; James 1:25). As an expression of His character, God's law cannot be changed any more than He can. His law is as perfect and unchanging as He is. That is why adultery, for example, is sin in every age and in every nation. God's standards of holiness and justice are universal and timeless.

2. The Presumption of Continuity

Since the law of God does not change, we can presume that it continues to apply unless God tells us otherwise. How, then, should we new covenant believers approach Old Testament laws? In view of recognized changes in the administration of the law from the Old Testament to the New, dispensationalists propose that we presume discontinuity—a radical break with the laws of the past. In other words, we should presume that no Old Testament commands remain valid unless they are explicitly repeated in the New Testament.[5]

But that approach to the law contradicts the first point above, namely that God's law expresses His perfect, unchanging character. If God's character remains the same, then His law remains the same.

Reformed theology teaches that Christians must presume continuity when approaching Old Testament commands. In other words, the commands of the Old Testament remain valid unless they are repealed in the New Testament. Since God

Himself is the Lawgiver, He is the only one who has the right to change the administration of His law. If we wish to remain faithful to God and to the authority of His Word, we must not presume changes in His Word unless He Himself reveals to us that He has made such changes.

Far from repealing the entire law, the Bible itself expressly presumes continuity between the Old and New Testaments. Although Lewis Sperry Chafer argues that Christ "disannulled" the law,[6] Jesus says in Matthew 5:17–19 that He did *not* come to abolish the law. Christ twice denies that the purpose of His coming was to abrogate the Old Testament commands. He announces in verse 19 that "whoever then annuls one of the least of these commandments, and so teaches others, shall be called least in the kingdom of heaven." But dispensationalism does not stop with the least of the commandments—it annuls them all!

If we take Jesus' words seriously, we must conclude that every law in the Old Testament remains valid until and unless God Himself cancels it. And the New Testament clearly indicates which kinds of laws no longer apply. The book of Hebrews, for example, expressly teaches that the ceremonial laws of sacrifice have been annulled because Jesus was the final sacrifice.[7] But Scripture nowhere indicates that the moral law as summarized in the Ten Commandments has been done away with.[8]

3. Moral Relativism

In its insistence that the law changes from age to age, dispensationalism falls into something similar to situation ethics. For example, Charles Ryrie writes: "What is law? The answer to that depends on what period of human history you are thinking about."[9] Insofar as Ryrie is saying that God's moral standards differ from one setting to another, that is moral relativism, and it is unbiblical. God's moral standards are absolute. They apply universally, to all people in all places at all times. Incest was wrong before Moses, it was wrong after Moses, and it is still wrong after Christ's first coming. It is wrong for an Israelite and for an Egyptian. It is wrong for a Christian and for a pagan. God's moral standards are absolute, timeless, and universal.

As we saw above, Ryrie states that "the law was never given to the Gentiles and is expressly done away for the Christian."[10] But that claim cannot be substantiated biblically. Throughout Scripture there is only one ultimate standard to which God holds not only Jews and but also "the stranger" among them (Lev. 24:22), "the nations" (Ps. 9:4–5), "the world" (vv. 7–8)— that is, Gentiles. Paul writes that "whatever the Law says, it speaks to those who are under the Law, that every mouth may be closed, and *all the world* may become accountable to God" (Rom. 3:19). God is the universal King over "all the earth," not only Israel (Ps. 47:2, 7–9). The "kings" and "judges of the earth" are commanded to worship the Lord (Ps. 2:10–12). In many other passages Scripture teaches that non-Israelites have the same moral standards as Israelites and that they are punished for breaking them (e.g., Lev. 18:24–27; 2 Kings 17:24–41; Ps. 119:118–19; Prov. 14:34; 16:12; 17:15; Isa. 10:1; 24:5–6, 15; Dan. 4:24–25; Amos 1:3, 6, 9, 11, 13; 2:1, 4, 6). All people of all ages and all nations are subject to the moral law of God. Dispensationalism's relativistic doctrine of the law implies that God has a double standard of justice.

4. The Mosaic Law Is God's Law

Dispensationalists often argue that God's law is not the Mosaic law but Christ's law.[11] But that distinction cannot be substantiated by Scripture. In the first place, God's moral law is one. He does not have more than one standard for obedience. His moral principles for our lives remain the same even when the outward administration of the law changes. Second, Jesus is God. The law revealed to Moses *is* Christ's law. It did not originate with Moses. It is not ultimately Moses' law but God's law *revealed* to Moses. Third, and most importantly, Scripture very often equates

God's law with the law of Moses (Deut. 30:10; Josh. 24:26; 2 Kings 10:31; 17:13; 21:8; 1 Chron. 22:12; 2 Chron. 6:16; 31:21; Ezra 7:6, 12, 14, 21; Neh. 8:8, 18; 9:3; 10:28–29; Pss. 78:1; 81:4; 89:30; 119:34, 77, 92, 97, 109, 174; Isa. 1:10; Jer. 6:19; 9:13; 16:11; 26:4; 31:33; 44:10; Dan. 6:5; Hos. 4:6; 8:1). The difference is not between the essence of the Mosaic law and the essence of the law of Christ. Both are the same law—the law of God. Even the law of love, rightly associated with Christ, was first given through Moses in Deuteronomy 6:5 as a summary of the Ten Commandments just revealed in chapter 5. The same moral law of God that was once administered under the old covenant is now administered under the provisions of the new covenant.

5. The New Covenant and the Law

We noted earlier that the new covenant was established with the death (and resurrection) of Jesus Christ. The new covenant is therefore being fulfilled in and by the church today.

Does this new covenant abrogate the Mosaic law and create a new law? On the contrary, Jeremiah 31:31–34 teaches that one of the provisions of the new covenant is that the law of God revealed to Moses on stone tablets will be written on the hearts of believers. O. Palmer Robertson explains, "God shall write his will on the fleshly tablets of the heart, in contrast with the older engraving of his law on stone tablets. But it will be essentially the same law of God that will be the substance of this engraving."[12]

The law of God under the new covenant is no longer external to us. That same law is now written on our hearts. In addition, the same Holy Spirit who writes the law on our hearts also indwells us and gives us the power to obey it (Ezek. 36:27). We fulfill the law to the extent that we walk in the power of the Holy Spirit (Rom. 8:4).

The difference between the old covenant and the new is not in the essence of the law itself. The difference is that under the old covenant administration, the law was external and man was unable to keep it. Under the new covenant administration, the law is written on believers' hearts and the indwelling Holy Spirit empowers them toward a more mature obedience than their old covenant forebears. But that obedience continues to be measured by the same rule of life—the moral law of God. Greg L. Bahnsen offers this summary of the Spirit's work in the believer's walk:

> If living by the Spirit indicates that salvation must bring sanctification, then it means that salvation produces a life of glad obedience to God's law. Salvation frees one from sin's bondage so that he can walk lawfully (James 1:25; Gal. 5:13–14), which is to say lovingly (cf. 1 John 5:1–3), for the leading evidence of the Spirit's work in one's life is love (Gal. 5:22). Those who have been saved by faith must be diligent to exercise the good works of love (Titus 3:5–8; James 2:26; Gal. 5:6), and the standard of good behavior and loving conduct is found in God's revealed law (Ps. 119:68; Rom. 7:12, 16; 1 Tim. 1:8; John 14:15; 2 John 6).[13]

6. The Old Testament Is Ethically Binding

Dispensationalists teach that the entire Old Testament is no longer ethically binding. In the words of Lewis Sperry Chafer, "The entire system, including the [Ten] commandments as a rule of life, ceased with the death of Christ."[14]

There are numerous problems with such a dismissal of the Old Testament. It raises dozens of questions that dispensationalists have been unable to answer, questions such as:

> If the validity of the law (or a portion thereof) has expired in the New Testament, as some claim, then what are we to make of scriptural assertions that God does not alter His covenant word, does not allow sub-

traction from His commandments, is unchanging in His moral character (which the law reflects), and does not have a double standard of right and wrong? Why then is the writing of the Old Testament law on our hearts central to the New Covenant? Why does the Bible say His commandments are everlasting? Why do New Testament writers say that the entire Old Testament is our instruction in righteousness and to be obeyed? Why do they cite its stipulations with authority and use them to bolster their own teachings? Why are we expected to model our behavior on Christ's, while we are told that He obeyed the law meticulously and perfectly? Why does the sanctifying work of the Holy Spirit entail the observance of God's law? Why does love summarize the law in particular? Why does faith establish the law for us to keep, and why does God's grace teach us to walk in the law's path of righteousness? Why are we told in numerous ways that the law brings blessings to those who heed it? Why are the law's requirements never criticized or explicitly repudiated in the New Testament? Why are those who do not keep the law but claim to know the Savior called liars? God's inspired word says all of these things and more. What reply can the detractors from God's law today make in the face of such insurmountable evidence of the law's full validity?[15]

Contrary to dispensationalism, the law is prominent in the teaching of Christ and the apostles (Matt. 4:7; 5:17–19; 6:10; 7:23; 12:5; 13:41; 15:4; 19:17–18; 22:40; 28:18–20; Mark 1:44; 2:25–28; 10:17–19; Luke 10:26; 11:42; John 7:19; 8:17; Rom. 6:12–13; 8:4; 13:9–10; 1 Cor. 7:19; 14:34; 1 Tim. 5:18; 2 Tim. 3:16–17; Heb. 8:4, 10; James 2:9; 1 John 3:3–5; 5:2–3; Rev. 12:17; 14:12). Moreover, the person who believes in the inspiration of the Old Testament must also believe in its abiding validity. The same Scripture that teaches the one also teaches the other. "All Scripture is *inspired* by God and profitable for teaching, for reproof, for correction, for training *in righteousness;* that the man of God may be adequate, equipped for every *good work"* (2 Tim. 3:16–17).

7. The Legitimate Functions of the Law

Though dispensationalists deny that there are any legitimate functions of the law today, traditionally theologians have recognized a threefold use of the law.[16]

1. *The Civil Use:* The law restrains sin and promotes righteousness in society.
2. *The Pedagogical Use:* The law convicts people of sin and convinces them of their inability to fulfill the demands of the law.
3. *The Normative Use:* The law serves as a rule of life for believers, guiding them in the way of righteousness.

The Bible reveals many legitimate functions of the law, all of which can be categorized under the three traditional uses. Bahnsen suggests ten:[17]

1. "The law *declares the character of God* and so reveals His glory" (Ps. 119; Matt. 5:22–48).
2. "The law *displays the demand* of God upon our lives as men" (Ex. 19:5–6; Lev. 20:7–8; Matt. 6:10).
3. "The law *pronounces blessing* upon adherence to its demands" (Deut. 10:13; Josh. 1:7; Pss. 1:1–4; 103:17–18; Matt. 6:33; Gal. 3:12; 1 Tim. 4:8).
4. "The law provides a *definition of sin"* (Rom. 3:20; 4:15; 5:13; 7:7; 1 John 3:4).
5. "The law *exposes infractions* and convicts of sin" (Rom. 7:9–14; Heb. 4:12).
6. "The law works to *incite rebellion* in sinful men" (Rom. 5:20; 7:8, 13; 8:7; 1 Cor. 15:56).
7. "The law *condemns all transgression* as deserving God's wrath and curse" (Rom. 4:15; 6:23; 2 Cor. 5:10; Gal. 3:10; Eph. 2:3; James 2:10; Jude 6; Rev. 20:12–15).

8. "The law *drives us to Christ* for salvation" (Rom. 3:19, 21–26; 5:18–21; 6:23; Gal. 3:23–24; Eph. 2:12).
9. "The law *guides the sanctification* of the believer" (Lev. 20:8; Ps. 119:24, 66, 105; Prov. 6:23; Rom. 8:4; 1 John 1:5–7; 2:3–6, cf. 3:4–10; 5:2–3).
10. "The law serves to *restrain the evil* of the unregenerate" (1 Tim. 1:9–10).

There is no scriptural basis for the dispensational rejection of the entire Old Testament law. God's moral standards do not change from age to age. In a relativistic age it is especially important to affirm that there are ethical absolutes, and God alone reveals them in His law. Dispensationalist leaders not only annul the Old Testament commandments but teach others to do likewise. In so doing, they are in direct violation of the teaching of our Lord Jesus Christ (Matt. 5:19).

NOTES

1. Charles C. Ryrie, *Balancing the Christian Life* (Chicago: Moody Press, 1969), 88.
2. See Lewis Sperry Chafer, *Grace* (Grand Rapids: Zondervan, 1922) and *Systematic Theology*, 8 vols. (Dallas: Dallas Seminary Press, 1947); also Charles C. Ryrie, *So Great Salvation* (Wheaton: Victor, 1989), and Zane Hodges, *Absolutely Free!* (Dallas: Redencion Viva, 1989).
3. John Murray, *Collected Writings of John Murray*, vol. 1, *The Claims of Truth* (Carlisle, Pa.: Banner of Truth, 1976), 196.
4. Chafer, *Grace*, 102.
5. Charles C. Ryrie, "The End of the Law," *Bibliotheca Sacra* (1967), 239–42.
6. Chafer, *Grace*, 88.
7. In one sense the ceremonial laws have eternal and unchanging significance, that is, insofar as they point to Christ. But now we fulfill them by faith in Christ Himself, whose finished work is the realization of all that the old covenant ceremonies foreshadowed.
8. The extent to which Old Testament judicial law pertains to us has been disputed among Reformed theologians. For further study of this subject see Greg L. Bahnsen, *Theonomy in Christian Ethics*, 2d ed. (Phillipsburg, N.J.: Presbyterian and Reformed, 1984 [1977]), and *By This Standard: The Authority of God's Law Today* (Tyler, Tex.: Institute for Christian Economics, 1985); William S. Barker and W. Robert Godfrey, *Theonomy: A Reformed Critique* (Grand Rapids: Zondervan, 1990); Greg L. Bahnsen, *No*

Other Standard (Tyler, Tex.: Institute for Christian Economics, 1991).

9. Ryrie, *Balancing the Christian Life*, 30.

10. Ibid., 88.

11. See, for example, Douglas J. Moo, "The Law of Moses or the Law of Christ," in *Continuity and Discontinuity* (Wheaton, Ill.: Crossway, 1988), 217.

12. O. Palmer Robertson, *The Christ of the Covenants* (Phillipsburg, N.J.: Presbyterian and Reformed, 1980), 281–82.

13. Bahnsen, *By This Standard*, 65.

14. Chafer, *Systematic Theology*, 7:225.

15. Bahnsen, *By This Standard*, 133–34.

16. Louis Berkhof, *Systematic Theology* (Grand Rapids: Eerdmans, 1939), 614–15.

17. Bahnsen, *By This Standard*, 192–200.

14

Lordship Salvation

Within the ranks of dispensationalism, a controversy has arisen concerning the nature of the gospel. For better or worse the debate has been labeled the "lordship salvation" controversy. It has divided dispensationalists into two camps: advocates of "lordship salvation," such as John MacArthur, and those who promote "nonlordship salvation," such as Charles Ryrie and Zane Hodges.

The controversy involves questions relating to the very nature of Christianity. What is the gospel? What is faith? What is justification? How can we have assurance of our salvation? These are not trivial questions. They must be answered and answered clearly. Unfortunately, in the heat of this debate, the answers have often been either clearly wrong or extremely confusing.

Three factors make a Reformed analysis of the "lordship salvation" controversy difficult. First, we must note that advocates of the nonlordship position are not in complete agreement with each other on every point. The two leading spokes-men for the nonlordship view, Zane Hodges and Charles Ryrie, differ on fundamental issues. Second, the best-known advocate of the dispensational lordship salvation position, John MacArthur, has modified his position since the publication of his first book on this subject. Third, both sides of the debate appeal to the Reformers for support, yet neither position is consistently Reformed.[1] Despite these obstacles, we must make an effort to clarify the important issues involved in this controversy.[2]

John MacArthur has listed seven fundamental points on which he, Charles Ryrie, and Zane Hodges find agreement.[3]

1. *The Cross.* "Christ's death on the cross paid the full penalty for our sins and purchased eternal salvation. His atoning sacrifice enables God to justify sinners freely without compromising the perfection of divine righteousness (Rom. 3:24–26). His resurrection from the dead declares His victory over sin and death (1 Cor. 15:54–57)."

2. *Justification by Faith.* "Salvation is by grace through faith in the Lord Jesus Christ alone—plus and minus nothing (Eph. 2:8–9)."

3. *Good Works.* "Sinners cannot earn salvation or favor with God (Rom. 8:8)."

4. *Prerequisites for Salvation.* "God requires of those who are saved no preparatory works or prerequisite self-improvement (Rom. 10:13; 1 Tim. 1:15)."

5. *Eternal Life.* "Eternal life is a gift of God (Rom. 6:23)."

6. *Immediate Justification.* "Believers are saved and fully justified before their faith ever produces a single righteous work (Eph. 2:10)."

7. *Believers and Sin.* "Christians can and do sin (1 John 1:8, 10). Even the strongest Christians wage a constant and intense struggle against sin in the flesh (Rom. 7:15–24). Genuine believers sometimes commit heinous sins, as David did in 2 Samuel 11."

There is no disagreement between MacArthur, Ryrie, and Hodges on the seven points above. They do, however, disagree on at least nine other important points. MacArthur lists repentance, faith, faith's object, faith's effects, salvation's extent, Christ's lordship, holy desires, assurance, and perseverance.[4]

In order to understand clearly the similarities and differences between the various positions, we shall examine each of the nine disputed points under four headings:

- The Radical Nonlordship Position (of Zane Hodges)
- The Moderate Nonlordship Position (of Charles Ryrie)
- The "Dispensational" Lordship Position (of John MacArthur)
- The Reformed Position

Our presentation of the Reformed position will include a brief critique of the nonlordship views.

1. Repentance

The Radical Nonlordship Position. Zane Hodges, former professor of New Testament studies at Dallas Theological Seminary, presents the case for the radical nonlordship position in several books. The most thorough exposition of his view is found in his book *Absolutely Free!*[5] There Hodges argues that repentance has absolutely nothing to do with salvation and should therefore never be included in the gospel message (AF 145–46).

The Moderate Nonlordship Position. Former professor of systematic theology at Dallas Theological Seminary, Charles Ryrie, makes the case for a moderate nonlordship position in his book *So Great Salvation.*[6] He contends that repentance is not a part of conversion but simply a change of mind about something. It is not meant to be a part of the gospel message (SGS 92, 99).

The "Dispensational" Lordship Position. John MacArthur sets forth the lordship-salvation position in his two books *The*

Gospel According to Jesus and *Faith Works: The Gospel According to the Apostles.*[7] He summarizes his understanding of repentance this way:

> The gospel calls sinners to faith joined in oneness with repentance (Acts 2:38; 17:30; 20:21; 2 Pet. 3:9). Repentance is turning from sin (Acts 3:19; Luke 24:47). It is not a work but a divinely bestowed grace (Acts 11:18; 2 Tim. 2:25). Repentance is a change of heart, but genuine repentance will effect a change of behavior as well (Luke 3:8; Acts 26:18–20). (FW 24)

The Reformed Position. Contrary to the views of both Hodges and Ryrie, the Bible often includes repentance in the gospel message (Acts 11:18; 17:30; 20:21). The Reformed doctrine of repentance may be summarized as follows:

(1) Repentance is a gift of God (Acts 5:31; 11:18; 2 Cor. 7:9–10; 2 Tim. 2:25).
(2) Repentance is turning to God, as well as a hatred of and turning from sin (2 Chron. 7:14; Job 42:6; Pss. 51:4; 119:128; Jer. 8:6; 15:7; 31:18–19; Ezek. 14:6; 18:30–31; 36:31; Joel 2:12–13, 15; Amos 5:15; Acts 20:21; 26:20; 2 Cor. 7:11; Rev. 9:20–21; 16:11).
(3) True repentance must not be confused with saving faith, but neither may it be separated from saving faith (Mark 1:15; Luke 13:3, 5; Acts 11:21; 20:21).
(4) True repentance bears good fruit (Matt. 3:8; Luke 3:8; Acts 26:20).

2. Faith

The Radical Nonlordship Position. Faith is simply belief in the truthfulness of certain facts (AF 31, 113). It only occurs at a single moment in time (AF 107, 111). It is solely a work of man, not a gift from God (AF 219).

The Moderate Nonlordship Position. Faith is primarily being convinced of the facts of the gospel, but it also includes an act of the will and an element of trust in a person (SGS 121, 156).

The "Dispensational" Lordship Position. "Salvation is all God's work. Those who believe are saved apart from any effort on their own (Titus 3:5). Even faith is a gift of God, not a work of man (Eph. 2:1–5, 8). Real faith therefore cannot be defective or short-lived but endures forever (Phil. 1:6, cf. Heb. 11)" (FW 24).

The Reformed Position. Hodges errs by not explicitly including in his concept of faith the notion of trust in a person. He speaks only of assent to the truth of statements. There is a great difference between believing *what* Jesus said and actually trusting in *Him* as a living person to save. The Reformed position includes both concepts:

(1) Saving faith is a gift of God, a result of the regenerating work of the Holy Spirit (John 6:44–45; Acts 13:48; 16:14; 18:27; 1 Cor. 2:4–5; 2 Cor. 4:6; Eph. 1:17–18; 2:8; Phil. 1:29).

(2) Saving faith includes both assent to the truth of the gospel and trust in the Lord Jesus Christ (Matt. 11:28; Mark 1:15; Luke 8:12; John 1:12; 6:35; 7:38; 11:26; Acts 9:42; 15:7; 16:31; 24:14; 26:18; Gal. 2:16, 20; 3:26; Col. 2:6; 1 Thess. 2:13; 2 Tim. 1:12; 3:15; Heb. 6:18; 10:23).

(3) Saving faith begins at a particular moment in time, at which point we are justified, and continues to live on. True faith cannot die (John 15:1–10; Gal. 2:20; Eph. 6:16; Phil. 1:6; Heb. 3:12–19; 10:35–39; 11:1–40; 12:1–2; James 2:14–26; 1 John 2:23; 5:4–5).

3. Faith's Object

The Radical Nonlordship Position. The object of faith is the collection of facts of the gospel message (AF 37, 39).

The Moderate Nonlordship Position. In contrast to Hodges,

Ryrie argues that the object of saving faith is the Lord Jesus Christ (SGS 121).

The "Dispensational" Lordship Position. "The object of faith is Christ Himself, not only a creed or a promise (John 3:16). Faith therefore involves personal commitment to Christ (2 Cor. 5:15). In other words, all true believers follow Jesus (John 10:27–28)" (FW 24).

The Reformed Position. Contrary to Hodges's radical view, the believer places his trust in a person, the Lord Jesus Christ, not only in truths about Him. According to the Reformed position:

(1) The object of saving faith in the general sense is the entire Word of God, all of which testifies of Jesus (Luke 24:27; Acts 24:14; 1 Thess. 2:13).
(2) The object of saving faith specifically is the person and work of Jesus Christ our Lord (Isa. 45:22; John 1:12; 3:15–16, 18, 36; 6:35, 37, 40; 7:38; Acts 10:43; 16:31; Rom. 3:22, 25; Gal. 2:16; Phil. 3:9).

4. Faith's Effects

The Radical Nonlordship Position. The only necessary effect of faith is salvation from the eternal penalty of sin. A life of continued growth in grace (progressive sanctification) and salvation from the power of sin are *not* necessary effects of faith (AF 75, 125).

The Moderate Nonlordship Position. In contrast to Hodges, Ryrie maintains that some fruit is inevitable in the true Christian life, though it may never be outwardly visible (SGS 45).

The "Dispensational" Lordship Position. "Real faith inevitably produces a changed life (2 Cor. 5:17). Salvation includes a transformation of the inner person (Gal. 2:20). The nature of the Christian is different, new (Rom. 6:6). The unbroken pattern of sin and enmity with God will not continue when a person is born again (1 John 3:9–10)" (FW 24).

The Reformed Position. Hodges again demonstrates the extreme nature of his doctrine by asserting that saving faith may have no effect on a Christian's life other than escape from hell. Ryrie's position, while not as extreme, does not adequately take into account that some visible fruit is necessary. How else are *we* to "know them by their fruits" (Matt. 7:20)? The Reformed position takes into account both effects:

(1) The first effect of our initial act of faith is justification (Rom. 3:25, 28, 30; 5:1; Gal. 2:16; Phil. 3:9).
(2) In addition, saving faith bears good fruit (Matt. 7:17–19; 12:33; Luke 6:44; John 15:1–11; Rom. 7:4; Gal. 5:19–23; Phil. 1:11).

5. Salvation's Extent

The Radical Nonlordship Position. Salvation means gaining eternal life. The other aspects of the Christian life are different kinds of "salvation," which believers must experience after conversion (AF 196).

The Moderate Nonlordship Position. Salvation guarantees justification and positional[8] sanctification but not necessarily progressive[9] sanctification (SGS 151).

The "Dispensational" Lordship Position. "The 'gift of God,' eternal life (Rom. 6:23), includes all that pertains to life and godliness (2 Pet. 1:3; Rom. 8:32), not just a ticket to heaven" (FW 24).

The Reformed Position. The nonlordship view in effect denies that every aspect of salvation—justification, sanctification, and glorification—was purchased for us at the Cross. The Reformed position takes each of these aspects of salvation into account.

God's gift of salvation includes far more than justification and eternal life (Rom. 8:30; 2 Peter 1:3). Salvation includes our faith and repentance, justification, sanctification, good works, resurrection, and glorification (Acts 5:31; 11:18; Rom. 3:25, 28, 30;

5:1; 1 Cor. 15:22–23, 42–44; Gal. 2:16; Eph. 2:8, 10; Phil. 3:21; Heb. 12:14).

6. Christ's Lordship

The Radical Nonlordship Position. There should be absolutely no aspect of submission to the lordship of Christ in the gospel message (AF 172).

The Moderate Nonlordship Position. A person can accept Jesus as Savior without acknowledging Him as the Lord of one's life and without being willing to allow Him control over one's life (SGS 74).

The "Dispensational" Lordship Position. "Jesus is Lord of all, and the faith He demands involves unconditional surrender (Rom. 6:17–18; 10:9–10). He does not bestow eternal life on those whose hearts remain set against Him (James 4:6)" (FW 25).

The Reformed Position. Nonlordship advocates believe a person can be saved without consciously submitting his life to Christ as Lord. Proponents of lordship salvation likewise recognize that most Christians were not conscious of every implication of the gospel when God saved them. But there is a vast difference between being saved despite a *limited awareness* of all the demands of Christ's lordship and being "saved" despite an *unwillingness* to submit one's life to Christ's lordship. Nonlordship teachers confuse these two situations. The result is that the visible church is now filled with people who only wanted Jesus as Savior but who never intended to submit to Him as Lord. The Reformed position maintains that:

(1) Jesus Christ is Lord; we do not make Him Lord (Acts 2:36; 10:36; 16:31; 20:21; Rom. 10:9).

(2) No one can have Christ as Savior without having Him as Lord (Phil. 2:10–11). If we have a Savior who is not the Lord, He is not the Christ of Scripture. The only one who saves is the Lord Jesus (2 Peter 3:18).

7. Holy Desires

The Radical Nonlordship Position. "The scriptural revelation knows nothing of a doctrine in which Christian love for God is guaranteed by the mere fact that one is a Christian" (AF 131).

The Moderate Nonlordship Position. Although Ryrie argues that "believers may live like unsaved people" for extended periods of time, he does not believe that this will be the lifelong state of any believer (SGS 31).

The "Dispensational" Lordship Position. "Those who truly believe will love Christ (1 Pet. 1:8–9; Rom. 8:28–30; 1 Cor. 16:22). They will therefore long to obey Him (John 14:15, 23)" (FW 25).

The Reformed Position. It is difficult to understand why Hodges would suggest that one can be a Christian and not love God. Scripture says, "If anyone does not love the Lord, let him be accursed" (1 Cor. 16:22). It is in the very nature of a Christian to love God, because He first loved us. Hatred of God is the nature of unbelievers. The Reformed position may be summarized this way:

(1) A true believer desires to obey God (James 2:18, 22; 1 John 2:4, 29; 3:7, 9–10).

(2) A true believer desires to stop sinning (Rom. 8:13; 1 John 2:9, 15; 3:6, 8, 15; 4:8).

8. Assurance

The Radical Nonlordship Position. Hodges argues that "when a person believes, that person has assurance of life eternal" (AF 50). And a continuous lack of fruit in a "believer's" life should never cause him to question his salvation (AF 93).

The Moderate Nonlordship Position. "The Bible offers two grounds for assurance. The objective ground is that God's Word declares that I am saved through faith.... The subjective ground relates to my experiences" (SGS 143).

The "Dispensational" Lordship Position. "Behavior is an important test of faith. Obedience is evidence that one's faith is real (1 John 2:3). On the other hand, the person who remains utterly unwilling to obey Christ does not evidence true faith (1 John 2:4)" (FW 25).

The Reformed Position. Ryrie, MacArthur, and many Reformed theologians agree that there is both a subjective and an objective basis for assurance. Hodges, however, refuses to allow for any subjective basis for assurance. According to the Reformed position:

(1) Objective assurance is conviction of the trustworthiness of Jesus Christ and His promises (Acts 16:31; Heb. 6:17–18). It asks, "Do you believe in Jesus Christ?"

(2) Subjective assurance is based upon inward evidences of true faith and the testimony of the Holy Spirit (Rom. 8:15–16; 1 John 2:3; 3:14). It is also based upon outward evidences of true faith, keeping God's commandments (1 John 1:6, 2:3–6, 9; 3:6, 10, 24; 5:2–5). It asks, "Is your faith real?"

9. Perseverance

The Radical Nonlordship Position. Hodges teaches that it is possible for a believer to cease believing and yet remain a Christian (AF 111).

The Moderate Nonlordship Position. Ryrie agrees with Hodges on this point. He argues that faith is a point-in-time action that may not continue in a Christian (SGS 141–42).

The "Dispensational" Lordship Position. "Genuine believers may stumble and fall, but they *will* persevere in the faith (1 Cor. 1:8). Those who later turn completely away from the Lord show that they were never truly born again (1 John 2:19)" (FW 25).

The Reformed Position. The doctrine of perseverance is the point at which the absurdity of the nonlordship position becomes very clear. According to both Ryrie and Hodges, a Christian can cease believing, become an atheist, and yet remain a Christian. We therefore have the possibility of unbelieving believers in the church. The Reformed position does not allow for this kind of absurdity:

(1) Those whom the Father has elected, the Son has redeemed, and the Spirit has called cannot totally or finally fall away from grace but will be eternally saved (Rom. 8:33–39; Phil. 1:6; Heb. 7:25; 1 Peter 1:5, 9; 2 Peter 1:10).

(2) Christians may fall into sin and continue in it temporarily, thereby bringing upon themselves God's discipline (2 Sam. 11:27; Pss. 32:3–4; 51; Isa. 65:5–9; Matt. 26:70–74; Mark 16:14; 1 Cor. 11:32).

(3) Saving faith begins at a particular moment in time, at which point we are justified, and continues to live on. True faith cannot die (John 15:1–10; Gal. 2:20; Eph. 6:16; Phil. 1:6; Heb. 3:12–19; 10:35–39; 11:1–40; 12:1–2; James 2:14–26; 1 John 2:23; 5:4–5).

Conclusion

Proponents of the nonlordship-salvation position have the worthy intention of preserving the doctrine of justification by faith alone. But that biblical doctrine becomes distorted when faith and repentance are redefined in an unbiblical manner. Yes, we are justified by faith alone. But that faith is a gift of God, a result of His life-giving work of regeneration. Just as the blind cannot see, and the deaf cannot hear, so too the spiritually dead cannot believe unless they are first made alive. It takes the miracle of regeneration to open our spiritual eyes, ears, and hearts. Only then do we see and hear and believe the truth. And it is all the gift of God.

Faith is more than a one-time-only event like the signing of an insurance policy. When God opens our eyes, we gain sight and go on seeing. When He opens our ears, we hear and continue to hear. And when He opens our hearts, we trust in Christ and continue to believe. Because saving faith is a supernatural gift of God, it cannot die. A "faith" that dies never was saving faith. Nor can a "faith" that bears no good fruit save. Our actions reveal the truthfulness of our words (Titus 1:16). If someone says he has faith but has no works, no fruit, or no love, his profession of faith is a lie. The Lord Jesus Christ offers complete salvation to all who genuinely trust in Him.

NOTES

1. Though MacArthur's "lordship salvation" position is largely Reformed, he has not renounced many of the dispensational errors we have discussed. The result is an unstable mixture of the Reformed gospel and dispensationalism. Since he continues to regard himself as a dispensationalist, this chapter will list his lordship views under the heading "The 'Dispensational' Lordship Position" (with quotation marks around "Dispensational"), notwithstanding his extensive agreement with the Reformed position.

2. Several good explanations of the "lordship salvation" controversy from a Reformed perspective are Richard P. Belcher, *A Layman's Guide to the Lordship Controversy* (Southbridge, Mass.: Crowne, 1990); Curtis I. Crenshaw, *Lordship Salvation: The Only Kind There Is!* (Memphis, Tenn.: Footstool, 1994); Kenneth L. Gentry, Jr., *Lord of the Saved* (Phillipsburg, N.J.: Presbyterian and Reformed, 1992); and Ernest C. Reisinger, *Lord and Christ* (Phillipsburg, N.J.: Presbyterian and Reformed, 1994).

3. John MacArthur, *Faith Works: The Gospel According to the Apostles* (Dallas: Word, 1993), 23-24.

4. Ibid., 215–17.

5. Zane Hodges, *Absolutely Free!* (Dallas: Redencion Viva, 1989). Because of space limitations, references to the books by Hodges, Ryrie, and MacArthur in this section will normally be parenthetical and will be included in the text. (AF) will refer to *Absolutely Free*, (SGS) will refer to *So Great Salvation*, and (FW) will refer to *Faith Works*. The page numbers will be included in the parenthetical reference.

6. Charles C. Ryrie, *So Great Salvation* (Wheaton: Victor Books, 1989).

7. John MacArthur, *The Gospel According to Jesus* (Grand Rapids: Zondervan, 1988); *Faith Works* (Dallas: Word, 1993).

8. "Positional" sanctification is the initial setting apart of a person to God at the moment of new birth.

9. "Progressive" sanctification is the Christian's growth in personal holiness that occurs throughout his or her life.

PART 4

The Dispensational Doctrine of the Last Things

CHAPTER 15

The Kingdom of God

Dispensationalism has long been known for its unique understanding of the kingdom of God. That is not to say that there has been total agreement among dispensationalists on all details concerning the kingdom. But there has been agreement on the essential doctrines.

In this chapter we will discuss four aspects of the dispensational doctrine of the kingdom: (1) the kingdom offer, (2) Jesus Christ's present kingship, (3) the throne of David, and (4) the heirs of the kingdom. The doctrine of the millennial kingdom will be discussed in greater detail in chapter 17.

The Kingdom Offer

Dispensationalism has traditionally taught that the purpose of Christ's first coming was to establish an earthly kingdom. Jesus, it is said, made a genuine offer of such a kingdom to the Jewish people, but the Jews rejected the kingdom offer. The kingdom was therefore postponed, and God began His new program with the church.

That is the view of all traditional dispensationalists. For example, Lewis Sperry Chafer says that the "setting up of Messiah's kingdom, though first faithfully offered to Israel, was deferred and now awaits the return of Messiah for its realization."[1] John F. Walvoord concurs: "It was in His offer to Israel as their King that He was rejected."[2] Charles Ryrie explains: "Throughout His earthly ministry Jesus' Davidic kingship was proffered to Israel (Matt 2:2; 27:11; John 12:13), but He was rejected. . . . Because the King was rejected, the messianic, Davidic kingdom was (from a human viewpoint) postponed."[3]

Some may doubt that this doctrine, taught by older dispensationalists, is still advanced today. But in 1990 J. Dwight Pentecost wrote:

> By stone and by storm, Satan carried on his relentless warfare in order to prevent Christ from coming to His appointed throne in the kingdom He had come to establish. . . . Jesus was officially presenting Himself as the covenanted Davidic king and was offering the covenanted kingdom to the covenanted people.[4]

If God intended that Christ establish an earthly Jewish kingdom, and Satan prevented that, then Satan defeated God. But Satan never defeats God. Had Jesus Christ come to establish an earthly Jewish kingdom, all the forces of heaven and hell combined could not have stopped God from accomplishing that purpose. The plans of God cannot be thwarted by man or Satan (2 Chron. 20:6; Job 42:1–2; Pss. 33:11; 135:6; Isa. 14:27; 43:13).

Jesus did not come in order to offer the Jewish nation an earthly political kingdom. He came to die (Matt. 20:28; Mark 10:45; John 13:3). Nor did the Jews reject an offer of an earthly political kingdom. That was exactly what they wanted. When they tried to make Him King by force, He wouldn't let them (John 6:15). Before the foundation of the world, God's plan and purpose was that Jesus Christ would suffer and die on a Roman cross for the sins of His people. That was the purpose of His first advent, and He perfectly accomplished what He came to do.

Is Jesus King Now?

Dispensationalists believe that since the Jews rejected Christ's kingdom offer, the kingdom is postponed and awaits the second coming of Christ to be established. Thus Jesus is not reigning as King in this age. Chafer explains, "One needs only to search the Scriptures to discover the fact that He [Jesus] is never mentioned as King of the church, nor even king of the nations until He comes again as 'KING OF KINGS, AND LORD OF LORDS' (Rev. 19:16)."[5] Ryrie agrees that Jesus Christ "does not rule as King [until] His second coming."[6]

The dispensational denial of Christ's present rule contradicts clear scriptural teaching. In the Great Commission Jesus said, "*All* authority has been given to Me in heaven *and* on earth" (Matt. 28:18). Paul and Silas caused an uproar because they taught that Jesus is King *now* (Acts 17:7). Elsewhere Paul writes that Christians have been transferred into Christ's kingdom (Col. 1:13). How can Christians presently be in the "kingdom of His beloved Son" if His Son is not now reigning as King?

A comparison of Acts 1 and Daniel 7 reveals that Jesus Christ has already been given His kingdom. Daniel 7:13–14 records Daniel's vision:

> I kept looking in the night visions,
> And behold, with the clouds of heaven
> One like a *Son of Man* was coming,
> And He *came up to the Ancient of Days*
> And was presented before Him.
> And to Him *was given dominion*,
> Glory and *a kingdom*,
> That all the peoples, nations, and
>   men of every language

Might serve Him.
His dominion is an everlasting dominion
Which will not pass away;
And His kingdom is one
Which will not be destroyed.

Dispensationalists consider this passage a prophecy of the second coming of Christ to earth to establish His millennial kingdom. But that is not what Daniel says. Verse 13 indicates clearly that this is not a vision of Christ's coming *down* to earth. Daniel sees the Son of Man coming *up* to the Father, the Ancient of Days. Daniel, writing from the perspective of one standing in the throne room of God, sees Jesus coming up. Daniel 7 cannot be a prophecy of the second coming.

Only one place in Scripture vividly describes the fulfillment of a scene like the one in Daniel 7. In Acts 1, Jesus Christ, the *Son of Man*, comes *up* to the Ancient of Days on the clouds (Acts 1:9). Daniel 7:13–14 is thus a prophecy of the ascension of Christ. In verse 14, we are told what happened after Christ ascended to the Father: He was given an everlasting dominion. He was given glory. He was given a kingdom that extends over all peoples, nations, and men of every language.

Despite dispensationalist denials, the Bible distinctly teaches that Jesus Christ was crowned King of Kings at His ascension. He is now "the ruler of the kings of the earth" (Rev. 1:5). "The kingdom of the world has become the kingdom of our Lord, and of His Christ; and He will reign forever and ever" (Rev. 11:15).

The Davidic Throne

Why do dispensationalists deny that Christ is reigning as King today? They do not accept His enthronement at the right hand of the Father as fulfillment of the promise that the King would sit on David's throne. J. Dwight Pentecost argues that "there is not one reference connecting the present session of Christ with the Davidic throne."[7] John Walvoord agrees: "If Christ is now on the throne of David, it is without any Scriptural support whatever."[8]

There are two glaring problems with that argument. First, Scripture, at times, virtually equates God's throne with David's (e.g., 1 Chron. 28:5; 29:23; 2 Chron. 9:8). Second, and more importantly, Scripture assures us that Jesus has already fulfilled the promises made to David. Peter's sermon in Acts 2 teaches that the promises were fulfilled when Christ ascended into heaven and was seated at the right hand of God. In Acts 2:30 Peter declares that David knew that God had sworn to seat one of his descendants upon his throne. In verses 31 and 34 Peter tells us that David looked ahead and saw that this promise would be fulfilled in Christ's resurrection and ascension. Dispensationalism is again in direct conflict with the inerrant Word of God.

The Heirs of the Kingdom

Dispensationalism teaches that the kingdom promises remain the sole property of national Israel and that these promises will only be fulfilled in the future millennium.[9] But is that what the Bible actually says?

In Matthew 21:43 Jesus speaks to the leaders of the unbelieving Jewish nation. He declares, "The kingdom of God will be taken away from you, and be given to a nation producing the fruit of it" (cf. Isa. 5:1–7). If it is taken away from the unbelieving nation of Israel, who is it given to? Jesus answers that question in Luke 12:32. Speaking to His disciples, He says, "Do not be afraid, little flock, for your Father has chosen gladly to give you the kingdom."

The kingdom, according to Jesus, has been taken away from the old Israel, national Israel. It has been given to the remnant, the new spiritual Israel, the church. Some may object that the church cannot be accurately termed a "nation" and therefore cannot be the nation Jesus refers to in Matthew 21:43. But Peter himself calls the church "a holy nation" in 1 Peter 2:9.

The church is the legitimate heir of the kingdom promises (Gal. 3:16, 29).

Conclusion

The dispensational doctrine of the kingdom must be rejected. It does not adequately acknowledge Christ's present reign as King. Christ's kingly office is made to wait until the millennium. But the Bible teaches us that Jesus is Prophet, Priest, *and* King now. He was given His kingdom when He sat down at the right hand of the Father. He is in the process of putting all of His enemies under His feet (1 Cor. 15:25). He is King of Kings and Lord of Lords today. All authority in heaven and earth is already His. To Jesus Christ the King be all glory and honor and dominion and power.

NOTES

1. Lewis Sperry Chafer, *Systematic Theology,* 8 vols. (Dallas: Dallas Seminary Press, 1947), 5:347.
2. John F. Walvoord, *Jesus Christ Our Lord* (Chicago: Moody Press, 1969), 282.
3. Charles C. Ryrie, *Basic Theology* (Wheaton: Victor, 1982), 259.
4. J. Dwight Pentecost, *Thy Kingdom Come* (Wheaton: Victor Books, 1990), 203–4.
5. Chafer, *Systematic Theology,* 5:341.
6. Ryrie, *Basic Theology,* 259.
7. Pentecost, *Thy Kingdom Come,* 144–45.
8. Walvoord, *Jesus Christ Our Lord,* 225.
9. See John F. Walvoord, *The Millennial Kingdom* (Grand Rapids: Zondervan, 1959), 172; Pentecost, *Thy Kingdom Come,* 173; and Charles C. Ryrie, *The Basis of the Premillennial Faith* (Neptune, N.J.: Loizeaux Brothers, 1953), 136.

CHAPTER 16

The Rapture

The most distinctive and best-known feature of dispensational eschatology is the doctrine that the church will be raptured out of the world prior to a seven-year period of worldwide tribulation. Many Christians today virtually equate belief in this pretribulation rapture with Christian orthodoxy. They assume that anyone who does not believe in a pretribulation rapture is a closet liberal, or worse. The truth is that most conservative Christians who do not believe in the pretribulation rapture reject it for valid scriptural reasons.

There is some controversy surrounding the origin of the doctrine of the pretribulation rapture. Although we cannot discuss its origin at length, suffice it to say that the doctrine was never taught before 1830. Nor is it found in the writings of any Christian author prior to the nineteenth century. Does that alone make the doctrine untrue? Not necessarily. But we should demand abundant and clear scriptural proof before accepting any doctrine that has eluded the church throughout its entire history. It is generally a good rule not to quickly embrace any new doctrine.

Do dispensationalists provide scriptural support for this admittedly new doctrine? As we shall see, the answer is no.

Pretribulationism Rests on the Dispensational Doctrine of the Church

John Walvoord, the most influential and best-known defender of the pretribulational rapture, openly admits that this doctrine is entirely inferential. It rests squarely on the dispensational doctrine of the church. Writes Walvoord, "It is safe to say that pretribulationism depends on a particular definition of the church."[1] He continues:

> If the term *church* includes saints of all ages, then it is self-evident that the church will go through the Tribulation, as all agree that there will be saints in this time of trouble. If, however, the term *church* applies only to a certain body of saints, namely, the saints of this present dispensation, then the possibility of the translation of the church before the Tribulation is possible [sic] and even probable.[2]

In this astounding admission, Walvoord bases his pretribulationism not on clear scriptural teaching but on a particular definition of the church—a definition we have already demonstrated to be unbiblical.

Walvoord himself admits that if the church includes the saints of all ages, then it is "self–evident" that the church will go through the Tribulation. He also allows that *even if* the dispensational definition of the church is true, pretribulationism is only "possible" or at best "probable." That is not a very strong foundation for a doctrine considered vital to dispensationalism. And since the dispensational definition of the church is biblically indefensible, it is no foundation at all. The person who believes in the pretribulational rapture needs to wrestle with this question: Why believe in a doctrine that originated in 1830 and is not based on any clear teaching of the Bible, but instead rests on another doctrine that is plainly unscriptural?

Even the other arguments in support of pretribulationism depend on the dispensational doctrine of the church. Unless that doctrine of the church is true, these secondary arguments are irrelevant. But in order to show that even these other alleged proofs do not support the pretribulational rapture, we shall examine several of them.

Other Alleged Proofs of Pretribulationism

1. The Wrath of God. It is often argued that pretribulationism finds support in passages that promise the church exemption from divine wrath. Not one of the passages cited (Rom. 5:9; Eph. 5:6; Col. 3:6; 1 Thess. 1:10; 5:9), however, provides explicit support for pretribulationism. The verses neither promise the church deliverance from tribulation generally nor specify a time of Great Tribulation. Each passage merely distinguishes between the fate of the saved and the fate of the lost.

Romans 5:9 teaches that because we have been justified by the death of Christ, we shall be saved from the wrath of God. What wrath? The context indicates that Paul means the wrath of hell, not a period of tribulation on earth. Ephesians 5:6 also addresses the fate of the unsaved. Paul says, "The wrath of God comes upon the sons of disobedience." This verse and the following verses speak of the eternal fate of unbelievers in contrast to the fate of the righteous. Colossians 3:6 similarly tells us that the wrath of God will come because of the sins mentioned in verse 5. Not one of these verses mentions anything that demands a pretribulation rapture.

First Thessalonians 1:10 tells us that Jesus is the one who delivers us from the wrath to come. What wrath is that? The wrath that has come upon the Jews (2:16). At the time of the writing of 1 Thessalonians, God had already begun to pour out

His judgment upon the generation of Jews that had crucified the Lord and persecuted the church. That wrath would soon be poured out in fullness upon Jerusalem in A.D. 70 when the Romans finally destroyed the city.[3] Jesus is also the one who delivers Christians from God's ultimate judgment, the wrath of hell. And 1 Thessalonians 5:9 simply contrasts wrath with salvation through Jesus Christ. It does not speak of the church's rapture out of a period of tribulation.

The scriptural message of all these passages is that the church is destined for salvation while the lost are destined for the wrath of God, both now and for eternity. These texts do not imply anywhere that the church cannot be present on earth when God is pouring out His vengeance on particular people at a particular time. In fact, God's people have often been present when He has poured out His wrath (e.g., Ex. 7–11).

Dispensationalists allege that one verse specifically promises the church exemption from a time of tribulation. Revelation 3:10, part of the letter to the church in Philadelphia, says, "Because you have kept the word of My perseverance, I also will keep you from the hour of testing, that hour which is about to come upon the whole world, to test those who dwell upon the earth." Dispensationalists argue that this verse teaches that the church cannot be present upon the earth during the Great Tribulation.

There are, however, several questions dispensationalists must answer before using this text to support pretribulationism. Where in this verse does Christ promise to remove the entire church physically from the earth? Where does it say that this verse refers to the end of the world? Doesn't it describe a period of testing that, at the time Revelation was written, was soon "about to come" (Rev. 1:3; 3:10–11; 11:14; 17:8; 22:6–7, 10, 12, 20)? If it does refer to a Great Tribulation at the end of the world, why is the Philadelphian church of the first century promised that they will be kept from it? They would all be long dead when it happened. If this specific promise to the Philadelphian church applies to the church at the end of this present age, why does the specific promise made to the church of Smyrna in Revelation

2:10 not also apply to the present-day church as a whole? Doesn't that verse say that the church will literally be cast into prison, die, and be given the crown of life?

Revelation 3:10 does not require the physical removal of the church from the earth during the hour of testing. In John 17:15 Jesus makes it very clear that one can be "kept from" evil without being "taken out of the world." He prays, "I *do not* ask Thee to take them out of the world, but to keep them from the evil one." Jesus expressly *contrasts* taking His church out of the world with keeping them from the evil one.

The two words Jesus uses in John 17:15 for "keep from," John again uses in Revelation 3:10.

John 17:15
<u>tereses</u> autous <u>ek</u> tou ponerou
"<u>keep</u> them <u>from</u> the evil one."

Revelation 3:10
<u>tereso ek</u> tes horas tou peirasmou
"will <u>keep from</u> the hour of testing"

Despite using the same words for "keep from" in both passages, John does *not* use the word for "take" in both. Had he wanted to speak of God's taking the church out of the world before a time of testing, it would have been natural for John to use the same language he did in John 17:15: *ares autous ek tou kosmou* ("take them out of the world"). But in Revelation 3:10 he avoids any mention of "taking" believers from the earth during a time of tribulation. He uses the word "keep" rather than "take." And, as we have seen, John sharply contrasted those two concepts in John 17:15, saying explicitly that Jesus' intention was *not* to take His people out of the world. Revelation 3:10 does not support the pretribulation rapture.

2. *The Use of the Word "Church" in Revelation.* Another line of argument used to support pretribulationism involves the nature and content of the book of Revelation. It is argued that since Revelation 4–19 depicts the Great Tribulation, and since the word *church* is not found in those chapters, the church is therefore not in the Tribulation. But this type of argument only leads to absurd conclusions. By the same reasoning we could say that the church will not be in heaven because the word *church* is not found in Revelation 20–22. In fact, Israel must also be raptured at some point because the word *Israel* is not found between 7:4 and 21:12. Better proof is needed to establish an important doctrine.

3. *The Distinction Between the Rapture and the Second Coming.* Dispensationalists argue that since the Bible talks about Christ's coming "for" the saints and "with" the saints, that implies two comings. The rapture, it is argued, is Christ's coming *for* His saints, and the Second Coming is Christ's coming *with* His saints. It is said that the difference between His coming *for* and His coming *with* the saints dissolves if the rapture and the Second Coming are simultaneous. Therefore the two comings must be kept separate.

If we examine the Scripture closely, however, we will see that the two words *for* and *with* present no real problem. Christ comes *with* the saints who have already died and *for* the saints who are still alive. The two occur at the same time, as a close look at 1 Thessalonians 4:14–17 reveals. Verse 14 tells us that "God will bring *with* Him [Christ] those who have fallen asleep"; and verse 17 teaches that Christ comes *for* those "who are alive and remain."

The argument that Christ will come *for* both the living and dead in verses 16 and 17 would prove too much. That would mean that believers who have died are not with Christ but instead remain in their graves. Scripture teaches, however, that Christians who have died are with the Lord (2 Cor. 5:6; Phil. 1:23). Verse 17 simply tells us that at the second coming of Christ, the *bodies* of the saints will be resurrected.

No text in the entire Bible tells us that God will rapture the church out of the world seven years before the second coming of Christ. Pretribulationism, as dispensational scholars themselves admit, rests entirely on their definition of the church. If that definition is wrong, then pretribulationism is wrong. If it is right, then pretribulationism is at best possible or probable. We have already demonstrated that the dispensational doctrine of the church is biblically indefensible. Where does that leave the doctrine of the pretribulational rapture? According to its most able defender, it means that pretribulationism must be self-evidently wrong.

NOTES

1. John F. Walvoord, *The Rapture Question*, rev. ed. (Grand Rapids: Zondervan, 1979), 21.
2. Ibid., 21–22.
3. Not only does pretribulationism depend on an indefensible definition of the church, it also depends upon the Great Tribulation being future. However, every passage of Scripture that explicitly mentions a great tribulation (e.g., Matt. 24:1–35; Mark 13:1–32; Luke 21:1–33) has been fulfilled in the judgment and destruction of Jerusalem in A.D. 70. See Appendix B; see also J. Marcellus Kik, *An Eschatology of Victory* (Phillipsburg: Presbyterian and Reformed, 1971); Gary DeMar, *Last Days Madness*, rev. ed. (Atlanta: American Vision, 1994); David Chilton, *The Great Tribulation* (Forth Worth: Dominion Press, 1987); Kenneth Gentry, *The Beast of Revelation* (Tyler, Tex.: Institute for Christian Economics, 1989).

CHAPTER 17

The Millennium

The time and nature of the millennium have been debated for almost two thousand years. Still there is no consensus among Bible-believing Christians concerning the millennium.

A person's doctrine of the millennium is not an indicator of orthodoxy the way other doctrines such as the Trinity and the deity of Christ are. Someone who does not believe in the Trinity is a heretic. But a person is not considered heretical simply on the basis of his or her millennial view. There can be differences among genuine Christians.

Two Varieties of Premillennialism

All dispensationalists are premillennialists. The essence of premillennialism is the belief that Jesus will return in order to establish His earthly kingdom, which will last for one thousand years. Put very simply, premillennialism fixes Christ's return *before* ("pre-") this thousand-year period ("millennium"). But premillennialism is not equivalent to dispensationalism. The essence of dispensationalism, as we have seen, is the radical distinction between the people of God of this age (the church) and the people of God of other ages (Israel, Tribulation saints, etc.)—they form not one body of believers but two or more.

Thus, while all dispensationalists are premillennialists, not all premillennialists are dispensationalists (e.g., George E. Ladd). There are both dispensational and nondispensational premillennialists. The disagreement between them centers not on the time of Christ's coming but on the nature of the millennial kingdom that Christ comes to establish.

Nondispensational premillennialism (also known as "historic premillennialism") maintains that Christ will establish an earthly kingdom and reign over the earth with His church. Dispensational premillennialism insists that the millennial kingdom will have a thoroughly Jewish nature. According to dispensational premillennialists, the primary purpose of the millennium will be the restoration of Israel. During the millennium God will fulfill all of the covenant promises He made to national Israel. Jesus will reign from David's throne in the city of Jerusalem. The temple will be rebuilt, and animal sacrifices will be reinstituted. Jerusalem and the nation of Israel will once again be given a place of prominence.

Premillennialism and the Doctrine of the Church

We noted in the previous chapter that pretribulationism rests entirely upon the dispensational definition of the church. To some extent, premillennialism also depends on this doctrine. John Walvoord explains, "To a large extent premillennialism, as well as pretribulationism, is dependent on the definition of the church, and premillenarians who fail to distinguish between Israel and the church erect their structure of premillennial doctrine on a weak foundation."[1] In other words, unless the dispensational doctrine of the church is true, the foundation of premillennialism is very weak.

J. Dwight Pentecost comments revealingly that if "the church fulfills this [the new] covenant, she may also fulfill the other covenants made with Israel and there is no need for an earthly millennium."[2] We have already seen in a wealth of New Testament passages that the new covenant is being fulfilled in and by the church (Luke 22:20; 2 Cor. 3:2–6; Heb. 7:22; 8:6–13; 9:15; 10:14–18, 29; 12:22–24). If that is true, then (in Pentecost's words) "there is no need for an earthly millennium."

The "Thousand Years" of Revelation 20:1–10

Any discussion of the millennial question would be incomplete without some consideration of Revelation 20:1–10. This is the New Testament passage that speaks of a thousand-year reign, a millennium.[3]

> [1]And I saw an angel coming down from heaven, having the key of the abyss and a great chain in his hand. [2]And he laid hold of the dragon, the serpent of old, who is the devil and Satan, and bound him for a thousand years, [3]and threw him into the abyss, and shut it and sealed it over him, so that he should not deceive the nations any longer, until the thousand years were completed; after these things he must be released for a short time. [4]And I saw thrones, and they sat upon them, and judgment was given to them. And I saw the souls of those who had been beheaded because of the testimony of Jesus and because of the word of God, and those who had not worshiped the beast or his image, and had not received the mark upon their forehead and upon their hand; and they came to life and reigned with Christ for a thousand years. [5]The rest of the dead did not come to life until the thousand years were completed. This is the first resurrection. [6]Blessed

and holy is the one who has a part in the first resurrection; over these the second death has no power, but they will be priests of God and of Christ and will reign with Him for a thousand years. [7]And when the thousand years are completed, Satan will be released from his prison, [8]and will come out to deceive the nations which are in the four corners of the earth, Gog and Magog, to gather them together for the war; the number of them is like the sand of the seashore. [9]And they came up on the broad plain of the earth and surrounded the camp of the saints and the beloved city, and fire came down from heaven and devoured them. [10]And the devil who deceived them was thrown into the lake of fire and brimstone, where the beast and the false prophet are also; and they will be tormented day and night forever and ever.

We must note two things about this passage that bear directly on the millennial question and dispensationalism. First, whatever else Revelation 20 may describe, it certainly does not describe the dispensational conception of the millennium. This is the only New Testament passage that refers to a millennial reign. But where in this passage do we find a single reference to the Jews, the nation of Israel, Palestine, Jerusalem, or the Temple? Nowhere. If these people and places are present, the passage is silent about them. That would be strange, considering that according to dispensationalists, the restoration of national Israel is the primary purpose of the millennium.

A second and more serious problem with a premillennial interpretation of Revelation 20 is that it disagrees with the end-time chronology established elsewhere in the New Testament. There are several end-time events plainly taught in Scripture. Such clear teachings should not be squeezed into an end-time chronology drawn from a less-clear text such as Revelation 20. Instead, more-obscure texts must be interpreted in the light of clearer texts. And the clearest texts tell us several things about the last days:

1. Paul teaches in 1 Corinthians 15:22–24 that the end immediately follows the resurrection of Christ's people at His coming (v. 24: "then comes the end").
2. Jesus informs us that this resurrection will occur on the "last day" (John 6:40).
3. Jesus also indicates that the resurrection of His people will be simultaneous with the resurrection of the wicked (John 5:28–29; 2 Thess. 1:6–10; cf. Dan. 12:2). An "hour" is coming, a point in time, when "all" will rise. The resurrection of the righteous and the resurrection of the wicked are not separated by a thousand years. Both occur on the Last Day.
4. Paul says that this resurrection spells the defeat and destruction of the last enemy, death (1 Cor. 15:26, 54–55).
5. John teaches that the destruction of the last enemy—death—takes place at the Great White Throne judgment, which follows the millennium (Rev. 20:11–14). The second coming of Jesus and the Great White Throne judgment, therefore, cannot be separated by a thousand-year period of time. Both occur on the Last Day, the day when all men are resurrected and death is destroyed.
6. Paul also informs us that on this Last Day Christ gives the kingdom over to the Father (1 Cor. 15:24). The Last Day is not the time when Christ receives the kingdom. It is when He hands it over to the Father. So the messianic kingdom must be prior to the Last Day, when Christ comes again.

A millennial age separating the second coming of Christ and the Great White Throne judgment does not fit into the New Testament picture of the last days. But if Revelation 20:1–10 does not describe a thousand-year period between the second coming and the final judgment, what period of time does it describe? We know that Revelation 20:1–10 describes the reign of Christ. And since Jesus was given His kingdom at His ascension, the "thousand years" must refer to the present age. If we carefully observe these verses, we will notice three scenes depicted. Two of these pertain to the entire present age, and one predicts an event at the end of the present age. They are:

(1) the binding of Satan (vv. 1–3).
(2) the reign of the saints with Christ (vv. 4–6).
(3) the rebellion of the wicked (vv. 7–10).

1. The Binding of Satan. The first three verses of Revelation 20 describe the binding of Satan. But how can we consider Satan to be bound in this age when he is obviously very active?

Several New Testament passages teach that Satan's power has been greatly restricted in this present age.

1. In Matthew 12:29, Jesus Himself refers to binding Satan so that He can plunder Satan's "house."
2. In Luke 10:18, Jesus responds to the disciples' report of casting out demons by exclaiming, "I was watching Satan fall from heaven like lightning."
3. In John 12:31, Jesus says that Satan shall be cast out as ruler of this world *now*—in His own day! He did not say Satan would be cast out thousands of years in the future.
4. Second Thessalonians 2:6–7 teaches that evil and lawlessness, the works of Satan, are currently being restrained.
5. Hebrews 2:14 tells us that "through death" Jesus rendered Satan "powerless."

Satan has clearly been bound in some sense in this present age. If the restrictive language of Hebrews 2:14 applies to his current activity, surely the language of Revelation 20 does also. Hebrews 2 speaks even more strongly of the binding of Satan than does Revelation 20. Satan is in a real sense "powerless" today because of the work of Christ. And that is essentially what Revelation 20 describes. Satan has been "bound" because of the work of Christ. His power has been greatly curtailed in this age. When Christ returns, the current limitation of Satan's power, accomplished by the death of Christ, will be completely realized because Satan will be cast into the lake of fire forever.

2. *The Reign of the Saints with Christ.* The second scene depicted in Revelation 20 is the saints' reign with Christ (vv. 4–6). This scene also describes the present age. As we demonstrated in chapter 15, Christ received His kingdom at His ascension. Jesus is reigning as King now (Acts 17:7; Rev. 1:5), and we are in His kingdom now (Acts 26:18; Col. 1:13). He must reign until He has put all enemies under His feet (1 Cor. 15:25). His reign is occurring now because the last enemy to be put under His feet will be death, which will happen at His second coming (1 Cor. 15:22–24, 26, 54–55; John 5:28–29; cf. Dan. 12:2; John 6:40; Rev. 20:11–14).

Christians also reign with Christ in this present age (Rev. 1:5–6; Rom. 5:17; Eph. 2:6). Those who reign with Christ are said to have a part in the first resurrection. But what is the first resurrection?

To answer that we must first ask, What is the first death? Throughout Scripture the first death is spiritual death (Gen. 2:17; Rom. 5:12; Eph. 2:1–3; Col. 2:13). The first resurrection, therefore, must be a spiritual resurrection or regeneration—the giving of new life to spiritually dead sinners. Regeneration is often spoken of in terms of resurrection (John 5:24; Eph. 2:5–6; Col. 2:12–13; 1 John 3:14). It occurs as we are united to Christ and made partakers of His resurrection (John 5:24; Rom. 6:5; Col. 3:1). The first resurrection in Revelation 20, therefore, is the believer's spiritual partaking of Christ's resurrection, rather than a future inauguration of a thousand-year millennium.

The apostle John writes of the two resurrections—one spiritual and one physical—in chapter 5 of his gospel. Verses 24–25 speak of spiritual resurrection, while verses 26–29 speak of physical resurrection. In Revelation 20:4 the same author speaks of the first resurrection in the same sense—spiritual life, regeneration. Only Christians have a part in the first resurrection.

The second resurrection occurs at Christ's second coming (1 Cor. 15:23). This resurrection is physical and includes all who are Christ's in the resurrection of life. All who are not Christ's are also raised at this time in the resurrection of condemnation (John 5:25–29; 6:40; Dan. 12:2). The Bible does not allow for a thousand-year separation between the resurrection of the just and the resurrection of the unjust. They are both raised on the Last Day.

3. The Rebellion of the Wicked. The third scene described in Revelation 20 is the rebellion of the wicked (vv. 7–10). Verse 7 begins where verse 3 ends. Whereas verses 1–3 describe the present age, verse 7 explains what will happen at the *end* of this present age. Satan will be temporarily released and will instigate a full-scale rebellion against the Lord. The rebellion will not last, however, because Satan and his rebels will be destroyed.

When Christ returns, the dead will be raised and judged. The last enemy, death, will be destroyed. Christ will have accomplished His purpose. He will have reigned and put all of His enemies under His feet, abolishing all rule, authority, and power. There will be a new heaven and a new earth, and Christ will deliver up the kingdom to God the Father. All things will be subjected to Christ, and Christ "will be subjected to the One who subjected all things to Him, that God may be all in all" (1 Cor. 15:24–28).

Objections

Many people argue that Revelation 20:1–10 cannot possibly describe this present age. There are two common objections.

1. What About the Thousand Years? Revelation 20 tells us of a period of time lasting a thousand years. But the present age has already lasted over 1900 years. How can it be the millennium of Revelation 20? The answer depends on whether John had in mind a literal "thousand years."

Numerous problems result from dispensationalists' insistence on taking the number literally. Consistency would seem to demand that dispensationalists take the number "one thousand" literally when it is used elsewhere in Scripture. But the results would be absurd.

For example, Deuteronomy 7:9 teaches us that God keeps His covenant and mercy with those who love Him and obey His commandments for a *thousand* generations. Abraham lived approximately four thousand years ago. He loved God and kept His commandments. We know that God has promised to keep His covenant with Abraham for a thousand generations. If a generation is forty years, then God must keep His covenant with Abraham for at least forty thousand years! That would leave at least thirty-six thousand years to go before this promise can be literally fulfilled! Many postmillennialists and amillennialists would have no problem with that, but few if any dispensationalists will allow for an interpretation that leaves us with another thirty-six thousand years of human history.

Psalm 50:10 teaches us that God owns the cattle on a thousand hills. Are there not far more than a thousand hills on this planet with cattle on them? Does this psalm literally mean that the cattle on hill 1001 belong to someone other than God? Of course not. The point is that in Scripture the number "one thousand" does not have to and often cannot be interpreted literally. The context must determine whether we ought take the number literally or not.

The context of Revelation compels us to interpret the number "one thousand" figuratively. The rest of the Bible indicates that the period described in these verses is the present age. There is no wicked rebellion in the future age *after* Christ hands over the kingdom to the Father (1 Cor. 15:24). And there is no thousand-year separation between the resurrection of the righteous and the Great White Throne judgment.

2. Doesn't Revelation 19 Speak of the Second Coming?
Some may ask how Revelation 20 can picture the age *before* Christ's second coming when it *follows* chapter 19, which seems to picture Christ's second coming. That is also a legitimate question. However, at least two points must be kept in mind when discussing the relationship between Revelation 19 and 20.

First, Revelation 19:17–20 describes a scene that is difficult to reconcile with Christ's second coming. The common dispensational interpretation is that the passage depicts a war between the human armies of earth and Christ, who is descending from heaven with His armies. According to Walvoord, "These armies of earth forget their differences and join in battle against the King of kings and Lord of lords."[4]

Several factors render that interpretation unlikely. Consider, for example, that Revelation 19:12 is John's description of the glorified Lord. It parallels the description of Christ in Revelation 1:17. But at that sight of the glorified Lord, John fell down in terror, though he was the beloved disciple. If the awesome sight of the glorified Lord fills a beloved Christian with terror, would it not have at least as fearsome an effect on His enemies?

When Christ returns there will be no resistance. Revelation 6:15–16 tells us how human soldiers react when faced with God's wrath.

> And the kings of the earth and the great men and the commanders and the rich and the strong and every slave and free man, hid themselves in the caves and among the rocks of the mountains; and they said to the mountains and to the rocks, "Fall on us and hide us from the presence of Him who sits on the throne, and from the wrath of the Lamb."

They will not rise up in bold resistance at the second coming of the Lord. They will cower in fear.

A second point to remember about Revelation 19 and 20 is that the text only reveals the order in which John *saw* the visions, not necessarily the order in which the events were to take place. Since events are described out of sequence elsewhere in the book of Revelation, it should be no surprise if they are not in sequence in chapters 19 and 20. For example, Revelation 11:17–18 speaks of Christ's reigning and the final judgment, but Revelation 12:1–6 describes a vision of His birth and ascension. The order of events is reversed. Since the visions in Revelation are not always in chronological order, and there is compelling evidence that Revelation 20:1–6 envisions the present age, it would be no problem even if Revelation 19 does describe the second coming.

Premillennialism is therefore left without sufficient scriptural support. Jesus Christ has received His kingdom and is reigning now from the right hand of God (Acts 2; Dan. 7:13–14; Acts 17:7; Col. 1:13; Rev. 1:5). His church is reigning with Him, both in heaven (Eph. 2:6) and on earth (Rom. 5:17; 1 Peter 2:9; Rev. 1:6). Christ will reign until He has put all of His enemies under His feet (Ps. 110:1; 1 Cor. 15:25). The last enemy to be destroyed will be death. That will occur on the Last Day, when Christ comes again (John 6:40; 1 Cor. 15:22–24). On *that* "day," at *that* "hour," there will be a resurrection of the righteous and a resurrection of the wicked (John 6:40; cf. 1 Cor. 15:26, 54–55). Since the day on which death is destroyed is also said to be the day of the Great White Throne judgment (Rev. 20:11–14), those two events cannot be separated by a thousand years.

Jesus Christ is King of Kings and Lord of Lords *today*. He is the Ruler over the kings of the earth (Rev. 1:5). The kingdom of this world has already become the kingdom of our Lord and of His Christ (Rev. 11:15; Dan. 7:13–14). He is in the process of putting all of His enemies under His feet. When that task is completed, He will return—*once and for all.* He will judge all men in righteousness, and He will deliver the kingdom to the Father.

NOTES

1. John F. Walvoord, *The Rapture Question*, rev. ed. (Grand Rapids: Zondervan, 1979), 20.
2. J. Dwight Pentecost, *Things to Come* (Grand Rapids: Zondervan, 1958), 116.
3. One of the best expositions of this text is that of J. Marcellus Kik in *An Eschatology of Victory* (Phillipsburg, N.J.: Presbyterian and Reformed, 1971). I am indebted to him for his many insights into this passage.
4. John Walvoord, *The Revelation of Jesus Christ* (Chicago: Moody Press, 1966), 278–79.

Conclusion

We have seen that the essential doctrine of dispensationalism is the radical distinction between the people of God in this age and the people of God of other ages. Dispensationalists hold that only believers in this age are the body of Christ.

We have discovered that view to be contrary to clear scriptural teaching. The key doctrine of dispensationalism—the doctrine that makes that system what it is—has no biblical support. Every other distinctive teaching of dispensationalism pivots on this unique doctrine of the church. Since the dispensational doctrine of the church lacks a biblical foundation, all the other doctrines that depend on it collapse to the ground.

In addition to an unbiblical doctrine of the church, dispensationalism has adopted a doctrine of salvation that violates Scripture by weakening the Bible's pronouncements concerning human sin. When sin is taken seriously, God's work in salvation is taken seriously, forcing us to fall on our knees in the grateful realization that we had no part in saving ourselves. But when people do not take sin seriously, enormous problems arise. A weakened doctrine of sin has produced within dispensationalism a diluted understanding of election, a doctrine of possible atonement, and the lordship-salvation controversy. The unusual eschatological doctrines of dispensationalists (doctrines such as the pretribulational rapture and, to a large extent, premillennialism) also stand or fall with their doctrine of the church. In fact, every doctrine that dispensationalists consider vital rests upon this unbiblical notion of the church rather than the clear teaching of Scripture.

True Christians are thus faced with a choice. The decision is whether to submit to the compelling witness of Scripture or to continue believing in a doctrinal system void of biblical basis simply because that system is what one has always been taught. I urge my dispensationalist brothers and sisters to consider this choice prayerfully, and to eagerly embrace the Word of truth.

Progressive Dispensationalism

The past fifteen years have witnessed some significant developments within the ranks of dispensationalists. Some dispensationalists have questioned and even discarded many of the
traditionally distinctive teachings of dispensationalism. They
have even gone so far as to reject the essential doctrine of
dispensationalism—its radical church-Israel distinction.

In my opinion this trend has both positive and negative
aspects. On the positive side, progressive dispensationalists have
moved closer to Reformed theology on a number of doctrines.
They now acknowledge that the kingdom has been inaugurated
and that there is a present as well as a future aspect of the
kingdom. They have also recognized the two-peoples-of-God
theory to be unbiblical, which, ironically, brings us to the negative side of progressive dispensationalism.

If the defining doctrine of dispensationalism is the two-
peoples-of-God theory, then to reject that theory is to reject
dispensationalism itself. "Progressive dispensationalism" is

therefore both an encouraging trend and a misleading or confusing title. The two-peoples-of-God distinction has been associated with dispensationalism since its beginnings in 1830. As recently as 1988 Craig Blaising, a progressive dispensationalist, observed that "among contemporary dispensationalists a general consensus exists that a distinction between Israel and the church is the essential distinguishing factor of dispensationalism."[1] Now in the preface of the book *Progressive Dispensationalism* Blaising notes that progressive dispensationalists have abandoned the two-peoples doctrine.[2]

In view of genuinely positive developments, how problematic is the name "progressive dispensationalism"? Perhaps an illustration will clarify my concern. Suppose I announced that I am a "progressive Baptist." When asked what that means, I explain that I have rejected believer's baptism by immersion only. I now believe that infant baptism is biblical and that the mode of baptism should be sprinkling or pouring. But I claim to be a progressive Baptist. What would a good Baptist tell me? He would remind me that believer's baptism by immersion only is the essence of what it means to be a Baptist. A person cannot reject those doctrines and honestly claim to be a Baptist, progressive or otherwise.

Similarly, suppose I have become convinced that Jesus will return *after* the millennium, not before it. Would I be honest to describe myself as a "progressive premillennialist." No. Or what if I have abandoned belief in God? Would I be a progressive theist?

Can a person believe that the Bible is full of errors and yet honestly claim to believe that Scripture is inspired? Can someone abandon every distinctive doctrine of orthodox Christianity, add a few man-made doctrines, and honestly claim to be a Christian? No, that is exactly what the cults do. Mormonism is not Christian simply because it claims to be. It denies the essence of Christianity. Liberals do the same thing. They redefine or deny the deity of Christ, the miracles, biblical inspiration, and the resurrection—yet they claim to be Christians.

The church suffers far too much damage when people do

not identify what they really believe. For the sake of accuracy, honesty, and understanding, "progressive dispensationalists" should no longer claim to be dispensational. Traditional dispensationalists would likely concur. Do most dispensational laymen realize that the "dispensationalism" now taught in their seminaries is not the dispensationalism they know? As much as I prefer to see Reformed theology taught in these seminaries, if someone is going to teach nondispensationalism in a dispensational seminary, students and donors should at least be aware of the fact. It is not enough to redefine the essential doctrines out of a system and call the resulting opposite teaching "progressive."

Progressive dispensationalism is not dispensationalism. But neither is it Reformed. Still unchanged are a number of its doctrines of salvation. For now, "progressive dispensationalism" is a generic form of premillennial, modified Arminianism. Its proponents are moving in the right direction in regard to the church and the end times. But honesty calls for us all to recognize that while they are not yet Reformed, neither can they any longer be rightly called "dispensational."

That is why this book has not interacted with the progressive dispensationalist position at any length. Even its own proponents disagree on what that position is because it is in a constant state of flux. To arrive at a consistent position they either must return to traditional dispensationalism, become historical premillennialists, or become Reformed. My hope and prayer is that they continue their journey toward Reformed theology. Since they have come a long way in that direction already, it only makes sense to discard the misleading title "progressive dispensationalism."

NOTES

1. Craig A. Blaising, "Development of Dispensationalism by Contemporary Dispensationalists," *Bibliotheca Sacra* 145 (July-September 1988): 273.
2. Craig A. Blaising and Darrell Bock, *Progressive Dispensationalism* (Wheaton, Ill.: Victor, 1993), 7.

APPENDIX

B

The Olivet Discourse

There has been an ongoing debate among dispensational scholars concerning the relationship between the rapture and the Great Tribulation. Will the rapture occur before the Great Tribulation (pretribulationism), after it (posttribulationism), or in the middle of it (midtribulationism)? Pretribulationism, as we have noted, depends entirely upon the dispensational doctrine of the church, and since that doctrine of the church is biblically indefensible, there is no biblical ground for a pretribulation rapture of the church out of this world.

Does that mean that the church will go through the Great Tribulation? No, but the reason for that may surprise some readers. The time of what is called the "Great Tribulation" is explicitly revealed by Jesus Christ in His discourse on the Mount of Olives, recorded in Matthew 24, Mark 13, and Luke 21. Jesus clearly prophesied that the events of the Great Tribulation would be fulfilled between A.D. 30 and A.D. 70, when Jerusalem was finally destroyed by the Roman army.[1] Thus, the reason why the church will not go through the Great Tribulation is that it already has.

The evidence for an A.D. 70 fulfillment of Matthew 24 is overwhelming. Verse 34 is crucial: "Truly I say to you, this generation will not pass away until all these things take place." Jesus is saying in this verse that everything He has previously prophesied (vv. 4–33) will take place before the generation to whom He is speaking passes away.

Some have argued that the word "generation" used here means not literally the generation but the race or nation to whom Jesus is speaking. In other words, Jesus is supposedly saying that the Jewish race will not pass away until all the things prophesied take place. That interpretation, however, collapses under the weight of scriptural evidence.

1. The phrase "this generation" is used five other times in Matthew (11:16; 12:41, 42, 45; 23:36). In every case it means the generation of Jews to whom Jesus was speaking, *never* race or nation.
2. The phrase "this generation" appears in the immediate context of Matthew 24:34. In 23:36, it clearly refers to the generation of Jews alive in A.D. 30. Matthew 24:34 refers to the same generation.
3. The phrase "this generation" in Matthew 24:34 occurs as part of a response to the disciples' specific question about the time of the destruction of the temple they had just left (24:1–3).

It seems more than clear from the text of Matthew 24 that Jesus fully expected everything He predicted in verses 4–33 to occur within approximately forty years. The context is so plain that it has led many liberal scholars to conclude that Jesus was mistaken. If the events Jesus prophesied in verses 4–33 did not occur in the first century, then the liberals are right: either Jesus was mistaken or Matthew was mistaken about what Jesus said. But neither of these alternatives is acceptable. There is a third option—Jesus was absolutely right in verse 34. All that He predicted in this passage did occur within forty years.

The reason so many Christians have a problem allowing "this generation" to mean Jesus' own generation is that most modern ears are unfamiliar with the language Jesus uses in verses 4–33. How, they ask, could such events have been fulfilled between A.D. 30 and 70? That is a legitimate question. In order to answer it, we must examine closely what Jesus says in Matthew 24:4–35.

Signs of Tribulation in Matthew 24:4–33

In verses 4–33, Jesus lists several signs associated with a period of severe tribulation. Notice that all of these signs occurred in the years leading up to the destruction of Jerusalem. There is nothing in these verses that did not happen between A.D. 30 and 70 and thus had to await later fulfillment in a future "Great Tribulation."

False Christs (24:4–5). Scripture and history testify that there were many who arose in the forty years following Jesus' death who were false christs (see, e.g., 1 John 2:18).

Wars and Rumors of Wars (24:6). Between A.D. 14 and 68 there were wars in Germany, Africa, Thrace, Gaul, Britain, Armenia, and elsewhere.

Famines (24:7). There were many famines between A.D. 30 and 70 (Acts 11:27–29; Rom. 15:25–28; 1 Cor. 16:1–5). The siege of Jerusalem resulted in a famine so severe that thousands died.

Earthquakes (24:7). History and Scripture record numerous earthquakes during this forty-year period (see, e.g., Acts 16:26). Among them were quakes in Crete, Smyrna, Miletus, Chios, Samos, Laodicea, Hierapolis, Colosse, Campania, Rome, Judea, and Pompeii.

Signs in the Heavens (Luke 21:11). "Signs from heaven" may be figurative language (see comments on v. 29, below), but even if it is literal, it was fulfilled. There was a comet in A.D. 60 during Nero's reign. Halley's Comet appeared in A.D. 66.

Tribulation and Persecution (24:9). The church lived through tremendous tribulation and persecution between A.D. 30 and 70. Peter and John were jailed (Acts 4:3). They were later flogged (5:40). Stephen was stoned to death (7:54–60). Persecution increased (8:1; 9:1). James was martyred (12:1–2). Paul was stoned almost to death (14:19). Both the Jews and the Romans ruthlessly persecuted Christians.

Apostasy (24:10). The Bible indicates that apostasy from the faith was widespread before A.D. 70 (Galatians, Colossians, 2 Tim 1:15; 4:10, 16).

False Prophets (24:11). There were many false prophets prior to A.D. 70 according to Scripture (Acts 20:29–30; 2 Cor. 11:13; 2 Tim. 2:16–18; 2 Peter 2:1–3; 1 John 4:1; 2 John 7).

Lawlessness (24:12). Scripture indicates a rise in lawless behavior at this time (1 Cor. 5:1–2; 2 Tim. 3:9). Caligula and Nero are just two prominent examples of lawless leaders.

The Gospel Preached to the Whole World (24:14). In verse 14, Jesus says that the gospel will be preached in the whole world. Was that fulfilled prior to A.D. 70? Scripture says yes. In Colossians 1:23 Paul says that the gospel "was proclaimed in all creation under heaven" (see also Rom. 10:18; Col. 1:6). By the time Paul wrote Colossians (around A.D. 60), he could say that the gospel had been proclaimed in all creation. Jesus' prophecy was fulfilled.

The Abomination of Desolation (24:15). A comparison of this passage with its parallel in Luke 21:20 reveals that the Abomination of Desolation consisted of the Roman armies' surrounding Jerusalem.

A Flight of Christians from the Siege (24:16–20). History records that during an unexpected and temporary Roman withdrawal from the siege on Jerusalem, most Christians fled the city. Many fled to the rock fortress of Pella about sixty miles northeast of Jerusalem.

Great Tribulation (24:21). The language Jesus uses here echoes references to horrible judgments throughout the Old Testament (see Ex. 11:6; Dan. 9:12; 12:1; Joel 2:2). For example, speaking of the destruction of Jerusalem by Babylon in 586 B.C.,

Ezekiel prophesied, "And because of all your abominations, I will do among you what I have not done, and the like of which I will never do again" (Ezek. 5:9). The language of Matthew 24:21, therefore, cannot refer to a one-of-a-kind, final judgment. It is common Old Testament judgment language.

False Reports of Christ's Coming (24:23–26). Jesus corrects the initial misunderstanding behind the disciples' question by telling them that when the judgment on Jerusalem begins, He will not be coming back visibly. The destruction of Jerusalem is a different kind of coming—a coming in judgment (see Isa. 19:1), not the Second Coming.

Why the Reports Are False (24:27–28). Verses 27–28 are a parenthetical statement. Jesus is essentially saying this: "Look, during this soon-coming judgment many are going to say that I have returned. Don't believe them. Because when I do return, there won't be any doubt. Everyone will know it. The destruction of Jerusalem (My coming in judgment) is a different event from My second coming. Don't expect me to come visibly during the judgment upon Jerusalem." Jesus' reference to the vultures in verse 28 refers to Jeremiah 7:33. Again He is using Old Testament judgment imagery.

The Sun, Moon, and Stars (24:29). The Old Testament often speaks of the darkening of the sun, moon, and stars in connection with judgment. Such language occurs many times in the prophets to refer to the historical judgment of nations.

- Isaiah 13:10—judgment of Babylon (539 B.C.)
- Isaiah 34:4—judgment of Edom (703 B.C.)
- Ezekiel 32:7—judgment of Egypt (568 B.C.)
- Joel 2:10—judgment of Judah (586 B.C.)
- Amos 8:9—judgment of the northern kingdom (722 B.C.)

The Son of Man (24:30). In verse 30, Jesus refers to Daniel 7:13–14, which is a vision of the ascension of Christ and His seating at the right hand of the Father (see also Matt. 26:64).

The Gathering of the Elect (24:31). The word translated angels (*aggelos*) may also mean "messengers," depending on the context. In Matthew 11:10, John the Baptist is referred to as an *aggelos*. The elect are gathered from the four corners of the earth through the preaching of the gospel by Christ's messengers (John 11:51–52; Rev. 7:9).

The Fig Tree (24:32–33). The sign of the fig tree is not the restoration of national Israel in 1948. That is evident when verse 32 is compared to its parallel, Luke 21:29. Luke says "the fig tree *and all the trees.*" The point is that the people to whom Jesus is speaking will know that the judgment is coming very soon when these signs begin to be fulfilled.

Transition

The Time Text (24:34–35). Verse 34 promises that all of these things will happen to the generation of Jews to whom He is speaking. In verse 35, He guarantees the prophecy by offering the emphatic assurance, "My words shall not pass away."

The Second Coming (24:36–25:46). There are at least six reasons why verses 34 and 35 should be considered transitional.[2]

1. Verse 34 is a concluding statement. If everything in chapters 24 and 25 was fulfilled in the first century, it would make more sense to place verse 34 at the very end. Everything after verse 34 is not a prophecy about "this generation."
2. There is a distinct contrast between what is near in verse 34 and far in verse 36—"this generation" versus "that day."
3. Before verse 34, the plural "days" is used. After verse 34, the singular "day" is used.
4. There are a multitude of signs of the coming in judgment before verse 34. There are no signs after verse 34. Before verse 34 false christs, earthquakes, famines, wars, and other such signs enable observers to know for certain that judgment is near (vv. 32–33). After verse 34, no

one can know (v. 36). It will be a complete surprise (vv. 39, 42, 44, 50).

5. Jesus claims He doesn't know the time of His second coming (v. 36). But He knows the time of the destruction of Jerusalem (24:6, 25, 29, 30, 34).
6. Before verse 34, there is a short time frame of forty years (v. 34). After verse 34, the time frame is long (24:48; 25:5, 19).

Conclusion

There is no biblical basis for pretribulationism. But this should not leave the church in perpetual fear of going through the "Great Tribulation." Scripture does not speak of an end-time Great Tribulation. Jesus' prophecy about tribulation in Matthew 24 was fulfilled between A.D. 30 and 70. That fulfillment should give us confidence that His promise to return again is true. All of his prophecies about the judgment of Jerusalem were fulfilled within one generation exactly as He said. We can be sure, then, that He will return again just as He promised.

NOTES

1. For further study see J. Marcellus Kik, *An Eschatology of Victory* (Phillipsburg, N.J.: Presbyterian and Reformed, 1971); Gary DeMar, *Last Days Madness*, rev. ed. (Atlanta: American Vision, 1994); R. T. France, *The Gospel According to Matthew*, The Tyndale New Testament Commentaries, ed. Leon Morris (Grand Rapids: Eerdmans, 1985).
2. Kenneth L. Gentry, Jr., "An Encore to Matthew 24," *Dispensationalism in Transition* 6, 5 (May 1993).

For Further Reading

Critiques of Dispensationalism

Allis, Oswald T. *Prophecy and the Church*. Phillipsburg, N.J.: Presbyterian and Reformed, 1945. A classic critique of dispensationalism focusing on the Israel-church distinction.

Bahnsen, Greg L. and Kenneth L. Gentry, Jr. *House Divided: The Breakup of Dispensational Theology*. Tyler, Tex.: Institute for Christian Economics, 1989. A response to and critique of *Dominion Theology: Blessing or Curse?* by H. Wayne House and Thomas Ice. Focuses on the dispensational doctrine of the law and of the last days.

Crenshaw, Curtis I. and Grover E. Gunn III. *Dispensationalism Today, Yesterday, and Tomorrow*. 3d ed. Memphis: Footstool, 1994. A comprehensive critique of dispensationalism by two former Dallas Theological Seminary students, with an emphasis on dispensational hermeneutics.

Gerstner, John H. *Wrongly Dividing the Word of Truth: A Critique of Dispensationalism*. Brentwood, Tenn.: Wolgemuth & Hyatt, 1991. A critique of dispensationalism, with an emphasis on dispensational soteriology.

LaRondelle, Hans K. *The Israel of God in Prophecy*. Berrien Springs, Mich.: Andrews University Press, 1983. Though written by a Seventh-day Adventist, this book is one of the best critiques of dispensationalism available. It is so devastating that dispensational authors avoid reference to it, even in footnotes.

Poythress, Vern S. *Understanding Dispensationalists*. 2d ed. Phillipsburg, N.J.: Presbyterian and Reformed, 1994. An interaction with recent developments in dispensationalism. The emphasis in this book is on hermeneutics.

The History of Dispensationalism

Bass, Clarence. *Backgrounds to Dispensationalism*. Grand Rapids: Eerdmans, 1960. A concise history of dispensationalism.

Blaising, Craig A. and Darrell L. Bock, eds. *Dispensationalism, Israel and the Church*. Grand Rapids: Zondervan, 1992. The introduction contains a brief overview of the history of dispensationalism.

Reformed Theology

Berkhof, Louis. *Systematic Theology*. Grand Rapids: Eerdmans, 1939. A standard twentieth-century Reformed theology textbook.

Calvin, John. *Institutes of the Christian Religion*. Library of Christian Classics, vols. 20–21. Trans. Ford Lewis Battles. Ed. John T. McNeill. Philadelphia: Westminster Press, 1960. The classic statement of the Reformed faith.

Hodge, Archibald A. *Outlines of Theology*. 2d ed. Carlisle, Pa.: Banner of Truth, 1972 (1879). An excellent introduction to Reformed theology in a question-and-answer format.

Hodge, Charles. *Systematic Theology*. 3 vols. Grand Rapids: Eerdmans, 1989 (1872). The *magnum opus* of this great nineteenth-century theologian.

Horton, Michael. *Putting Amazing Back into Grace*. Grand Rapids: Baker, 1994 (1991). An excellent introduction to Reformed theology.

Sproul, R. C. *Essential Truths of the Christian Faith*. Wheaton, Ill.: Tyndale House, 1992. A clear and concise overview of Reformed theology.

Turretin, Francis. *Institutes of Elenctic Theology*. 3 vols. Trans. George Musgrave Giger. Ed. James T. Dennison, Jr. Phillipsburg, N.J.: Presbyterian and Reformed, 1992–95. A masterful Reformed classic recently made available in English.

The Westminster Confession of Faith and Catechisms.

The Doctrine of the Church

Bannerman, James. *The Church of Christ*. 2 vols. Edmonton, Alta.: Still Waters Revival, 1991 (1869). The most complete statement of the Reformed doctrine of the church available.

Kuiper, R. B. *The Glorious Body of Christ*. Carlisle, Pa.: Banner of Truth, 1967. A concise introduction to the doctrine of the church.

The Doctrine of Salvation

General Works on Reformed Soteriology

Boettner, Loraine. *The Reformed Doctrine of Predestination*. Philadelphia: Presbyterian and Reformed, 1963. This classic is the best introduction to Reformed soteriology available.

Buchanan, James. *The Doctrine of Justification*. Carlisle, Pa.: Banner of Truth, 1961 (1867). This book is the best statement of the doctrine of justification, even after 130 years.

Calvin, John. *Calvin's Calvinism*. Trans. Henry Beveridge. Grand Rapids: Eerdmans, 1950.

Hoekema, Anthony. *Saved by Grace*. Grand Rapids: Eerdmans, 1989.

Murray, John. *Redemption: Accomplished and Applied*. Grand Rapids: Eerdmans, 1955. One of the best introductions to the doctrine of redemption.

Palmer, Edwin H. *The Five Points of Calvinism*. Enl. ed. Grand Rapids: Baker, 1980.

Spencer, Duane. *TULIP: The Five Points of Calvinism in the Light of Scripture*. Grand Rapids: Baker, 1979.

Steele, David N. and Curtis C. Thomas. *The Five Points of Calvinism*. Phillipsburg, N.J.: Presbyterian and Reformed, 1963.

Warfield, Benjamin B. *The Plan of Salvation*. Boonton, N.J.: Simpson, 1989 (1915).

Total Depravity

Boston, Thomas. *Human Nature in its Fourfold State*. Carlisle, Pa.: Banner of Truth, 1964 (1720).

Edwards, Jonathan. *Freedom of the Will*. Ed. Paul Ramsey. New Haven, Conn.: Yale University Press, 1957.

Luther, Martin. *The Bondage of the Will*. Trans. J. I. Packer and O. R. Johnston. Westwood, N.J.: Revell, 1957.

Murray, John. *The Imputation of Adam's Sin*. Phillipsburg, N.J.: Presbyterian and Reformed, 1959.

Unconditional Election

Boettner, Loraine. *The Reformed Doctrine of Predestination*. Philadelphia: Presbyterian and Reformed, 1963.

Calvin, John. *Calvin's Calvinism*. Trans. Henry Beveridge. Grand Rapids: Eerdmans, 1950.

Sproul, R. C. *Chosen by God*. Wheaton, Ill.: Tyndale House, 1986.

Thornwell, James H. *Election and Reprobation*. Philadelphia: Presbyterian and Reformed, 1961.

Definite Atonement

Hodge, Archibald A. *The Atonement*. Grand Rapids: Eerdmans, 1953.

Morris, Leon. *The Apostolic Preaching of the Cross*. Grand Rapids: Eerdmans, 1955.

Owen, John. *The Death of Death in the Death of Christ*. Carlisle, Pa.: Banner of Truth, 1959 (1648). This classic work deals with every conceivable Arminian objection to the biblical doctrine of the atonement. It remains unanswered after 350 years. The introduction by J. I. Packer is an excellent introduction to the subject.

Smeaton, George. *The Apostles' Doctrine of the Atonement*. Carlisle, Pa.: Banner of Truth, 1991 (1870).

————. *Christ's Doctrine of the Atonement*. Carlisle, Pa.: Banner of Truth, 1991 (1870). This volume and the one above exhaustively discuss every passage in the New Testament dealing with the atonement.

Irresistible Grace

Kuyper, Abraham. *The Work of the Holy Spirit*. Trans. Henri DeVries. New York: Funk & Wagnalls, 1900. An invaluable classic.

Owen, John. *The Holy Spirit: His Gifts and Power*. Ed. George Buirder. Grand Rapids: Kregel, 1954. A masterpiece.

Smeaton, George. *The Doctrine of the Holy Spirit*. Carlisle, Pa.: Banner of Truth, 1974 (1889).

The Perseverance of the Saints

Boettner, Loraine. *The Reformed Doctrine of Predestination*. Philadelphia: Presbyterian and Reformed, 1963.

Palmer, Edwin H. *The Five Points of Calvinism*. Enl. ed. Grand Rapids: Baker, 1980.

Steele, David N. and Curtis C. Thomas. *The Five Points of Calvinism*. Phillipsburg, N.J.: Presbyterian and Reformed, 1963.

The Christian and the Law of God

Bahnsen, Greg L. *By This Standard: The Authority of God's Law Today.* Tyler, Tex: Institute for Christian Economics, 1985. An excellent antidote to dispensational antinomianism.

Bolton, Samuel. *The True Bounds of Christian Freedom.* Carlisle, Pa: Banner of Truth, 1964 (1645). A Puritan classic.

Gentry, Kenneth L., Jr. *God's Law in the Modern World: The Continuing Relevance of Old Testament Law.* Phillipsburg, N.J.: Presbyterian and Reformed, 1993.

Kevan, Ernest. *The Grace of Law.* Ligonier, Pa: Soli Deo Gloria, 1993 (1965).

Strickland, Wayne G., ed. *The Law, the Gospel, and the Modern Christian.* Grand Rapids: Zondervan, 1993. See the chapters by Bahnsen and Kaiser.

Lordship Salvation

Belcher, Richard P. *A Layman's Guide to the Lordship Controversy.* Southbridge, Mass.: Crowne, 1990.

Crenshaw, Curtis I. *Lordship Salvation: The Only Kind There Is!* Memphis, Tenn.: Footstool, 1994.

Day, R. Alan. *Lordship: What Does It Mean?* Nashville: Broadman Press, 1993.

Gentry, Kenneth L., Jr. *Lord of the Saved: Getting to the Heart of the Lordship Debate.* Phillipsburg, N.J.: Presbyterian and Reformed, 1992. An excellent refutation of the nonlordship position.

Horton, Michael S., ed. *Christ the Lord: The Reformation and Lordship Salvation.* Grand Rapids: Baker, 1992. An analysis of this dispensationalist controversy from a distinctly Reformed perspective.

MacArthur, John. *Faith Works: The Gospel According to the Apostles.* Dallas: Word, 1993.

Reisinger, Ernest C. *Lord and Christ: The Implications of Lordship for Faith and Life.* Phillipsburg, N.J.: Presbyterian and Reformed, 1994.

The Doctrine of the Last Things

The Rapture

Chilton, David. *The Great Tribulation*. Fort Worth, Tex.: Dominion Press, 1987. This book demonstrates that the Great Tribulation occurred in A.D. 70.

DeMar, Gary. *Last Days Madness*. Rev. ed. Atlanta: American Vision, 1994. An excellent analysis of the hysteria often associated with dispensational speculations about the end of the world. Includes a preterist exposition of Matthew 24.

Kik, J. Marcellus. *An Eschatology of Victory*. Phillipsburg, N.J.: Presbyterian and Reformed, 1971. The best exposition of Revelation 20 available, and one of the best expositions of Matthew 24.

MacPherson, Dave. *The Incredible Cover-Up*. Medford, Ore.: Omega, 1975. An interesting examination of the origins of pretribulationism.

North, Gary. *Rapture Fever*. Tyler, Tex.: Institute for Christian Economics, 1993. Examines the religious and societal consequences of total preoccupation with the rapture.

The Millennium

Brown, David. *Christ's Second Coming: Will It Be Premillennial?* Edmonton, Alta.: Still Waters Revival, 1990 (1876). A premillennial convert to postmillennialism explains why premillennialism is biblically indefensible.

Campbell, Roderick. *Israel and the New Covenant*. Phillipsburg, N.J.: Presbyterian and Reformed, 1981. A neglected study of the church and the new covenant in relation to eschatology.

Gentry, Kenneth L., Jr. *He Shall Have Dominion*. Tyler, Tex.: Institute for Christian Economics, 1992. An excellent presentation and defense of postmillennialism.

Grenz, Stanley. *The Millennial Maze*. Downers Grove, Ill.: InterVarsity Press, 1992. The best concise presentation of the different millennial views. Stanley is amillennial.

Scripture Index